I Heard Good News Today 3:
Faith Adventures With God

In Partnership With

By: Charissa Roberson
with Dan Hitzhusen

ii

Published by Mission Minded Publishers in the United States for UnveilinGLORY in partnership with e3 Partners. Copyright © 2016. The illustrations inside were designed by Bob Sjogren and Charissa Roberson and created by Markus Benyamin Diredja.

This publication may not be reproduced, stored in a retrieval system, or transmitted in whole or in part in any form or by any means, electronic, mechanical, photocopying, recording, or otherwise without prior written permission of Mission Minded Publishers.

> With the huge success of *I Heard Good News Today 2: Big Life*, Debby and I have teamed up with Charissa Roberson once again to work on this third *I Heard Good News Today* book chronicling the acts of the Holy Spirit through Dan Hitzhusen and other faithful believers.
>
> "We did this," says Debby, "because we wanted to give kids a vision of how God can use them in sharing their faith. Having taken homeschoolers overseas on mission trips ourselves, we have seen how easy it is for young people to share the gospel using the EvangeCube."
>
> Bob has known Dan for over two decades and he is very aware of how God uses Dan. Knowing this, he asked Dan if UnveilinGLORY and e3 Partners could team up to get these stories out to others. Dan was more than open to the idea.
>
> As the idea was formalized, Charissa and her parents flew out to San Diego to hear the stories from Dan. All three came back blown away by how God moved so greatly through Dan and others on e3 Partners' short-term mission trips to bring so many into His Kingdom. You'll also read fascinating stories of how others led their friends and family into God's kingdom with the EvangeCube.
>
> These are just a few of Dan's many stories. I hope this book encourages you to share your faith more freely as well as experience the great joy that follows. But watch out, these stories may also get you to consider going on an e3 trip with Dan!
>
> Bob Sjogren

e3 PARTNERS
equip. evangelize. establish.

All of the stories on the following pages
are true stories.
They've come about
because God loves to speak through
ordinary people yielded to His Spirit.

As you read these stories,
we hope you, too,
yield to God's Spirit inside of you.
As you do this,
we pray that you'll touch
hundreds, if not
thousands, of others
with the good news.

A Personal Letter From Dan

Dear Readers,

God has called believers to share the gospel of the Kingdom to people in every tribe, tongue and nation. He has commissioned us and we get the great privilege of declaring His Glory and showing His awesome love to people.

My hope as you read this book is that you come to realize we serve an awesome God who leads and guides us through His Word, His Spirit, and His people to do mighty miracles today. I work with a wonderful ministry called e3 Partners and we have taken over 50,000 thousand people on short-term mission trips throughout the world. The stories in the book exemplify ordinary people being used by an extraordinary God to do and see amazing things happen for His Kingdom.

Each of these stories is true. Some of the names have been changed for security purposes. All of the stories happened to either me personally or to people e3 Partners has taken on short-term mission trips. Several times you will hear references to an evangelism tool called the EvangeCube. An EvangeCube is simple visual tool that opens and folds in unique ways to share the gospel. Search for it on YouTube and you can see how to use it.

It has been a true joy for me to work with Charissa Roberson who is such a gifted writer and sweet sister in Christ. I believe God is going to use her greatly to make a positive difference in this world. Also, I am so grateful for my friendship and partnership in the Kingdom with Bob and Debby Sjogren.

But I want you to know that I wasn't always excited about sharing my faith. I came to know and trust Jesus personally when I was a senior in high school. I went away to college at the University of Tennessee to study business in hopes of making millions of dollars. As I grew to love and know God, my heart changed from making millions of dollars to helping people come to know the joy found only in a relationship with Jesus Christ.

When I graduated from the University of Tennessee I joined Campus Crusade for Christ (Cru) staff, specifically working as a personal assistant for author and speaker, Josh McDowell. Over the next few years Josh and I traveled to more than 20 countries and 300 cities around the world. It was an amazing experience to see God at work particularly in places where Christians are highly persecuted.

After going on my first short term trip with e3 Partners to Mexico, my heart was so changed that I went on staff with e3 Partners ministry. My wife, Lorie, and I have been serving with them for more than 20 years.

In those years, we have taken our three kids, Jonathan, Joshua and Kimberly on multiple trips starting when they were 8, 9 and 10 years old. What a joy to watch our kids minister the love of Christ to others at such a young age! In fact, e3 Partners has a special ministry called e3 Legacy that specializes in families going on mission together. Maybe you could pray about taking a trip with your family overseas with e3 Partners!

Perhaps one of the greatest pleasures and privileges of my life has been to work side by side with national believers, many of whom have put their lives on the line for the sake of the gospel. They are true heroes of the faith and God has special rewards stored up in heaven for these dear brothers and sisters in Christ.

Our prayer for you is that this book will challenge your heart to step out in faith and trust God for supernatural things. If you do, you'll find something very interesting happen. In Luke 10:1-17, Jesus sent out 72 of his disciples on their own short-term mission trip. What resulted? The 72 returned with joy, saying, "Lord, even the demons are subject to us in your Name!"

It is my prayer that you will see a theme of joy running throughout this entire book. It is this joy that I have experienced that I want you to have as well.

As e3 Partners leads close to two hundred short-term mission trips a year, we would love to take you with us. You can find out more information at www.e3partners.org.

My dear readers, God has commanded us to go into the entire world and make disciples. As you read these stories, remember that God has stories like these waiting for you. He created you for good works. As you go, God will get all the glory, and you will get the joy of building His Kingdom—empowered and commissioned by the King of Kings!

Hoping to build your faith—and your joy,

Dan Hitzhusen
International Vice President, e3 Partners

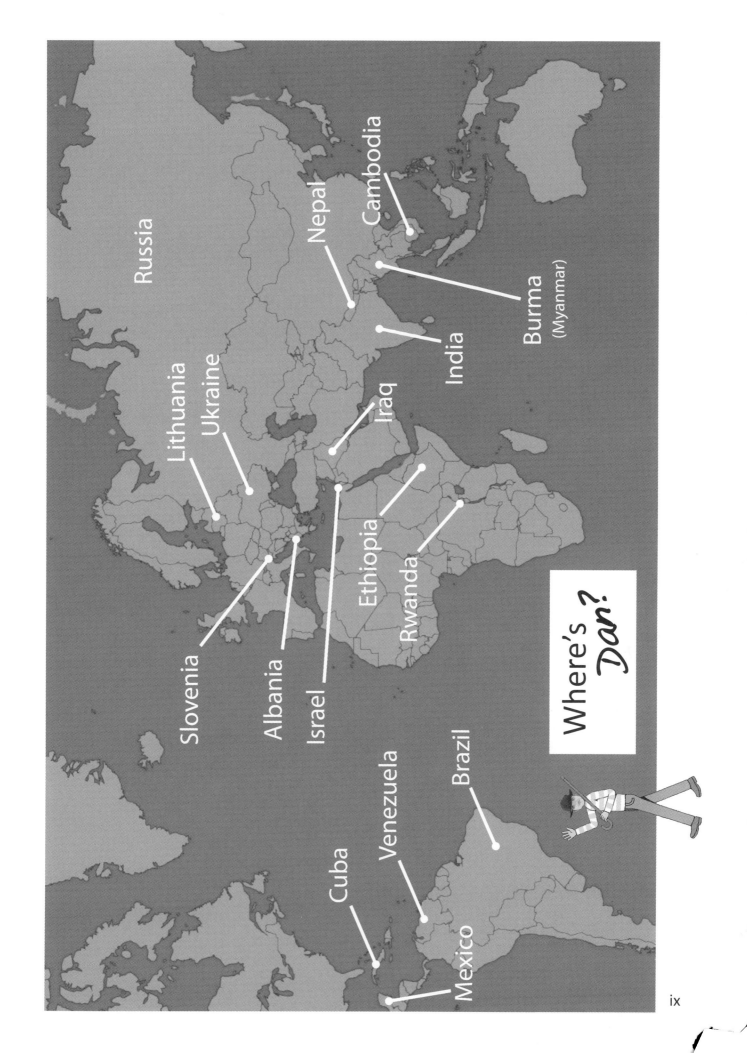

Table of Contents

Chapter 1: Below the Dogs 1
Chapter 2: No Contacts? No Problem! 5
Chapter 3: From Faith to Faith 9
Chapter 4: It's a Miracle 11
Chapter 5: Caught on Camera 15
Chapter 6: I See Love 17
Chapter 7: Two Fish 19
Chapter 8: To India by Faith 23
Chapter 9: The Terrorist Village 27
Chapter 10: No Matter What the Cost 29
Chapter 11: A Wild Ride 33
Chapter 12: In a Place Without God 37
Chapter 13: Into the Lion's Den 39
Chapter 14: A Time to Dance 43
Chapter 15: My Best Friend Jesus 47
Chapter 16: The 28 Day Journey 49
Chapter 17: Unexplainable 51
Chapter 18: The Greatest Miracle 55
Chapter 19: The Hotel Church 57
Chapter 20: The Power to Save 59
Chapter 21: The Face of Jesus 63
Chapter 22: Somebody Town 67
Chapter 23: A Break in Enemy Lines 69
Chapter 24: Let's Just Play 71
Chapter 25: You Look Like Jesus 75
Chapter 26: Forgiven 77
Chapter 27: The Future in His Hands 79
Chapter 28: You Have Not Because You Ask Not 83
Chapter 29: Duckling Discipleship 85
Chapter 30: A Meeting with Mother Teresa 87
Chapter 31: He Saw Me 91
Chapter 32: By the Dark of Night 93
Chapter 33: Keep On in the Lord's Work 95
Chapter 34: Protection or Destruction? 99
Chapter 35: Interrogation and the Secret Police 103
Chapter 36: Painting Targets 105
Chapter 37: The Two Swords 107
Chapter 38: Let's Pray Again 111
Chapter 39: Chicago? 115
Chapter 40: The Book of Acts in Action 117

Chapter 41:	Beyond Languages	119
Chapter 42:	Tell Them Why We're Here	123
Chapter 43:	Like We Love Ice Cream	127
Chapter 44:	Freedom Behind Bars	129
Chapter 45:	Do You Believe the Same as Billy Graham?	133
Chapter 46:	God of the Storm	135
Chapter 47:	Commencement Address	139
Chapter 48:	A Strategic Photograph	143
Chapter 49:	And God Stopped the Hurricane	147
Chapter 50:	Say Yes	149
Chapter 51:	A Way In	151
Chapter 52:	Two Prayers, One Answer	153
Chapter 53:	At the Right Time	155
Chapter 54:	Midnight Miracle	157
Chapter 55:	A Chess Game, the gospel, and The King	159
Chapter 56:	The Most Important Thing Ever	161
Chapter 57:	Down the Jungle Path	165
Chapter 58:	A Letter to the Island of Youth	167
Chapter 59:	Five-Minute-Old Believers	169
Chapter 60:	A Symbol of Salvation	171

Below the Dogs

"Lord," Dan prayed as he looked at the refuse all around him, "there are 26 million people in Mexico City—why did we have to come *here*?"

It was Dan and Lorie's first trip with e3 Partners. A year earlier, a team had come down to partner with a local church in Mexico City, whose desire was to plant 50 churches in the 50 districts of Chimalhuacan—a community outside of Mexico City. The Christians had succeeded in planting 10 churches during that time, and now another e3 team had come to try to help the Mexicans plant even more.

But Chimalhuacan was not a place where Dan would have picked to do ministry.

Years ago, Chimalhuacan had been a swamp. But as Mexico City grew larger, the swamp was transformed into the city's garbage dump. Tons of garbage and junk had been thrown into Chimalhuacan. Then someone decided to turn Chimalhuacan into a community where people could live. A foot of dirt was laid down over the vast ocean of stinking, disgusting trash. Houses were built, and Chimalhuacan was now home to four million Mexicans.

All the garbage lying just beneath the soil made the air foul and steamy; orange gases rose from the earth as the junk moved into deeper and deeper stages of decomposition. Open sewers fermented on the street corners, sending sour clouds of stench into the hot breeze. The people lived in waste and poverty. Their clothes were dirty and smelly. The e3 team was afraid to even touch the people because disease was continually circulating in the district.

Again, as the team stepped into Chimalhuacan, Dan asked, "Lord—why here?"

Dan and Lorie walked close together down the streets, following their team leader. It was difficult to breathe. There seemed to be no fresh air anywhere. The people, dirty and greasy, watched the team as they walked into the community. Their eyes were hollow and vacant.

They passed by a street vendor on the side of the road who was selling what looked like fried chicken feet. Out of curiosity, Dan examined the delicacies closer. Yuck. He grimaced, his stomach turning in revulsion. They were fried chicken feet, and they were covered with flies.

"Care for some French fries?" he whispered to Lorie. She glanced towards the vendor and immediately looked away, trying not to gag.

The trip taxed Dan and Lorie with its various unsavory challenges, though none topped that of their teammate, the wife of e3 Partners' founder, who actually fell into one of the open sewers. By the end of the first day, Dan was exhausted and so, so ready to get out of Chimalhuacan and back to fresh air, clean beds, and *a shower*. But then he thought of the Mexican missionaries—from the church in Mexico City—who had left their comforts and clean homes to *live* in Chimalhuacan. Their passion to reach the people for the Lord and to plant churches in the community was amazing. The disease and filth didn't scare them off; they embraced it. Dan felt a little ashamed for wanting to go home after such a short time.

A couple of days into the trip, Lorie and Dan came across a lone woman on the outskirts of the community. She walked beside a makeshift cart which was pulled by a short, tired-looking donkey. With her shoulders slumped and her face downcast, the woman shuffled by wearily. She was wrapped in a ragged, dirty jacket and, like all the residents of Chimalhuacan, her skin was coated with grease and grime. Her cart was piled high with garbage. She had been scavenging in the pits and piles around the community, looking for anything resembling food or anything she could use or sell or trade. This was the only way she could survive.

Lorie walked up to her. "Hello," she said in a friendly tone. "My name is Lorie."

The woman gazed at Lorie as if unable to believe that she was addressing her. "My name is Maria," she said finally.

"My friends and I have come to share God's good news," Lorie went on. "Would you like to hear about Jesus?"

Maria didn't respond. She stayed where she was, listening. Lorie told her about Jesus, God's Son, who had died for sinners. But even as Lorie was speaking, Maria started shaking her head. There were tears in her eyes.

"Jesus can't love me," she said quietly. "I am below the dogs here."

Lorie stopped, her heart aching for this woman who had no idea how much she was loved. Lorie moved closer and took Maria's hands.

"Jesus loves everyone," Lorie said firmly, "including those who are outcast and lonely. He loved you enough to come to earth and die in your place. He wants to save you. He wants to make you his child."

Maria stared at Lorie. Her hands were shaking and her tears smudged the dirt on her face. "How can I know Him?" she whispered.

Lorie led Maria in a prayer to accept Christ as her Savior. Dan stood nearby, watching. He heard Maria's humble, awe-filled prayer to Jesus, asking Him to take away her sins and be her Lord. And he saw her as she opened her eyes and raised her head. She was smiling.

The eyes that had been empty and hopeless were now alight with life. She hugged Lorie, laughing with joy. She knew she was loved. She knew Jesus would never abandon her. She knew that though society thought of her as beneath even the dogs, Jesus had accepted her as His precious daughter.

As Dan watched, he felt his eyes begin to sting. God loved these people with a blazing passion. He wanted to claim them as His own. He wanted His people, Christians, to love them in the same way He did.

When the e3 team completed their week of ministry in Chimalhuacan, several people had come to Christ and a church had been planted in the district. Dan and Lorie and the others no longer stayed away from the people for fear of illness. They shook hands with them and hugged them and prayed with them. They gave them all the clothes in their suitcases so they could have new, clean garments to wear. Dan received the answer to his prayer. *Why here?* Because God so loves the world.

This mission trip with e3 Partners became the first of many for Dan. He joined e3 Partners' staff and began leading teams of his own all around the world. But the memory of that first trip to Chimalhuacan always stayed fresh in Dan's mind. Even years later, he still got tears in his eyes when he remembered how, in the midst of the stinking, rotting garbage dump, the radiant beauty of God had shone on Maria's face.

No Contacts? No Problem!

"There's the world," one of the staff of e3 Partners said to Dan when he joined their organization. "Go get' em, tiger!"

They didn't give Dan any specific instructions on where to begin working across the globe. Their only advice was for him to go, share the gospel, and plant churches. So Dan had to think: where should he start trying to reach out? There were hundreds of countries waiting, needing to hear the gospel. But which one did God want him to go to first?

Israel held a special place in Dan's heart. While traveling with Josh McDowell, Dan had been baptized in the Jordan River. That memory was strong and precious to him, and the rich history and breathtaking aura of the Holy Land drew him. Dan decided he would go back to Israel and try to start working with the Messianic Jews.

Before Dan could bring a team over or start any kind of ministry, he had to make connections with the Christian nationals in Israel. Their counsel and guidance would be invaluable to the work, and their partnership was indispensable. There were so many things Dan had no idea about, while the Israelis, who actually lived in the country, were much wiser and capable.

Dan and his wife, Lorie, traveled together on this journey to establish relationships with the Israeli believers. First on their agenda in Israel was an opportunity to speak to 600 Arab Christians. However, due to an overnight delay in Paris, they missed the meeting. Dan and Lorie were discouraged. But trusting God's plan, they boarded their flight to Israel the next morning.

"Let me help you with that," Dan said hastily, as an older woman struggled to push her luggage into the overhead compartment.

"Thank you," she said gratefully, stepping aside. Dan helped her stow her bags, and then they both sat down. The older woman was sitting in the same row with Dan and Lorie. As the plane took off and began the flight to Israel, the three of them started chatting. Dan and Lorie explained why they were traveling to Israel. When they expressed their desire to find contacts in Israel, the woman's eyes lit up.

"I must introduce you to my son-in-law," she said excitedly. "He's picking me up at the airport. He is the pastor of a Messianic congregation in Israel. He would love to know about your ministry!"

Dan and Lorie exchanged glances. Could this be their first contact, while they were still en route to Israel?

The plane landed safely some hours later. Dan helped the woman unload her bags, and then together the three of them went to meet her son-in-law. He was waiting as they emerged from security.

With a broad smile, he hugged his mother-in-law and took her bags from her.

"I met this couple on the plane," she said to him, gesturing towards Dan and Lorie. "They are looking for people to partner with to do evangelism and church planting in Israel. I told them about your church."

"Come visit us anytime," he said cheerfully. He pulled a card from his pocket and handed it to Dan. "We meet at 40 Bethlehem Street, Jerusalem."

The group said their goodbyes as Dan spotted Philip, the Arab national who was picking them up from the airport, moving through the crowd.

With a final wave to the woman and her son-in-law, Dan and Lorie hurried towards Philip.

Philip greeted them and shook their hands. "Come," he said, "my car is out this way."

Philip took Dan and Lorie to his home in Haifa There they stayed at his house with his wife and seven children. They spent many hours in conversation with Philip and some Southern Baptist missionaries, talking about starting work in Israel.

A short while into their stay, Philip received a phone call from Nazareth.

"Sure, I would love to come," Philip said to the caller, barely concealing a delighted grin.

When Philip hung up, he instantly turned to Dan and Lorie. "They're having a church planting conference in Nazareth," he said. "I don't suppose you'd want to come?"

Dan nodded quickly, staring at Philip in amazement. What better place to find contacts for church planting, then at a church planting conference?

They all attended the conference in Nazareth, and while there Dan and Lorie were able to form relationships with several people and share their vision with them. They exchanged contact information with the Israelis and said they would be in touch.

After the church planting conference in Nazareth, Dan and Lorie went to Jerusalem and Bethlehem. Dan knew a man named Bill who owned two homes across from the Jaffa Gate, and Bill had offered Dan and Lorie the hospitality of staying there while they searched for contacts in Jerusalem and Bethlehem.

One quiet afternoon, Dan and Lorie were walking the streets of Bethlehem. The ancient buildings rose breathtakingly against the sky. Along the streets, men in long robes were walking slowly, or talking with their fellows. Several vendors declared their wares from the street corners.

Lorie paused by a table filled with olive wood carvings. Admiringly, she let her eyes travel over the rich, shiny wood, skillfully shaped into various forms.

The man's craftsmanship was so impressive, and the olive wood so beautiful, that Dan and Lorie couldn't resist buying a piece. They purchased a statue of Moses from the seller, whose name was Mohsen. Mohsen was a Muslim. He lived in the area and carved olive wood at his workshop just outside of the city. He was delighted to share his work with Dan and Lorie.

In a short period of time, all three became good friends. Mohsen took it upon himself to be Dan and Lorie's guide around the Old City. He showed them the best places to visit, and where to shop, and how to get the greatest deals.

As they walked with Mohsen through the city, he suddenly began waving excitedly.

"Homer! Mimi!" he said. He hurried to meet a couple who was coming down the street towards him. Homer and Mimi's faces broke into huge smiles as they saw Mohsen. The three friends hugged each other warmly.

"Come meet Dan and Lorie," Mohsen said, motioning Homer and Mimi over.

Dan and Lorie shook hands with Homer and Mimi. The little group began to talk, and Dan and Lorie found out that Homer and Mimi were missionaries working in the Golan Heights to reach the Lebanese and Druze peoples. Then, Homer and Mimi revealed that they were good friends with the Narkis Street Baptist Church, which was a church with which Dan and Lorie were hoping to partner. Homer and Mimi were also close friends with a man named Victor Bloom, who was working to reach Russian Jews.

This one encounter had given them even more contacts. The number of incidents, people, and meetings that God had presented to them during the course of the trip was overwhelming. But God wasn't done, even yet.

Late one afternoon, Dan and Lorie were enjoying a walk through Jerusalem. They talked casually about family and friends and the work that God was doing in Israel. Suddenly, Dan stopped walking.

"Hey!" he said. "It's Wednesday!"

Lorie looked at him oddly. Dan whipped out a card from his pocket and waved it in the air. "That's the day that this Messianic congregation has their service. Remember the guy at the airport, the woman's son-in-law—he's the pastor."

"Where is the church?" Lorie asked, peering over Dan's shoulder.

"40 Bethlehem Street," Dan read off the card.

Jerusalem was a huge city, with a population of half a million people, and hundreds of streets and hundreds of buildings. Dan and Lorie had simply gone wandering into the city. They looked up to the street sign they were standing under.

It read: "30 Bethlehem Street."

Dan laughed out loud. "It's only a block away!" He glanced at the card again. "And the service starts in five minutes."

Grinning at each other, Dan and Lorie walked off down the street. One block over, they arrived at the church just before the service started. There, Dan and Lorie visited with the pastor and talked with several other people in the congregation, forming relationships and making connections with their ministry.

And before Dan and Lorie left Israel, they met a man named Avi. He was the head of all the Messianic congregations in Israel. But he also happened to run a book shop in Tel Aviv, which was where Dan and Lorie ran into him and became introduced. Unknown to them at the time, God would use this "chance" relationship with Avi more than 10 years later to reach people in Iraq for Christ.

Every happening on their trip—from a missed flight, to helping a woman with luggage, to their encounter with Mohsen, to winding up on 30 Bethlehem Street at just the right time—had been orchestrated by God to establish the work Dan and Lorie were hoping to do in Israel. It was a journey of discovery; all they had to do was follow God's leading, and He had taken them exactly where He wanted them to go.

From Faith to Faith

A year after their search for contacts, Dan and Lorie had returned to Israel for their first outreach trip with a team of 11 people. The national missionaries had welcomed them at Haifa Baptist Church, the congregation with which Dan and his team were partnering. Then the missionaries had given the team an orientation to try to familiarize them with all the people they would be encountering.

"If you are speaking with a Muslim, there is a certain way to present the gospel," the missionary said. "However, if you are speaking with a nominal Arab, you should use a different approach. Then, if you meet a Druze man..."

Dan stared helplessly at his notebook. Finally he closed it and put his pencil away. There was no way he could remember all the different methods of sharing the gospel. How in the world were he and his team going to be able to interact with all these different people groups?

As he listened to the missionary explain how to have a conversation with a Russian Jew, all he could think was: *There's no way, God. There's no way we can possibly do this—only You can.*

After the orientation, Dan gathered his whole team for prayer and together they submitted themselves to God. "Lord," Dan prayed, "We are completely lost. You are the only one who can accomplish this task. Please, do it." After finishing the prayer, Dan told his team, "Let's go with the basics of God's Word—look for your person of peace and let them open doors for you."

The group of missionaries at Haifa Baptist Church split into two teams; one began outreach in Haifa, and the other, which Dan led, traveled to Mt. Carmel to share the gospel. Dan's team began ministry in a town called Isofia. The team went from door-to-door, hoping to talk with the people about Jesus. But few people wanted to listen.

Then Dan noticed something—at every house they went to, his interpreter was greeted by name. She was an extremely outgoing, loud-spoken, cheerful girl from Haifa Baptist Church who lived in Mount Carmel. Her name was Diana. She knew *everyone* in the community, and everyone knew her. Dan realized that she was their "person of peace." He asked Diana if she would lead them through the community and take them to the houses where she had relationships. Diana happily agreed.

The team began following a new pattern. Diana would take them to the house of someone she knew, knock on the door, and greet the people there. Then she would introduce the American missionaries. Because Diana opened the door, quite literally, the team was able to meet many families and share the gospel with many people. By the end of the week, directly through Diana's personal relationships, 29 people in Isofia came to Christ.

When the week of outreach was over, the team set up a church service to celebrate. It was a simple, rustic affair—really only a bunch of plastic chairs set out on the side of the road. A small crowd of people arrived, and the team spent time worshiping with them.

Near the start of the service, an unfamiliar man came up and found a seat. He listened quietly as the worship and speaking went on. He seemed to be contemplating something, deep inside.

Dan was listening to one of his teammates share a testimony when a loud shout startled him. The whole crowd fell silent. Spinning around, Dan saw a priest stumbling into the rows of chairs. He had a bottle of liquor in one hand and a cigarette in the other. As he staggered forward, he waved the bottle in the air and shouted loudly in Arabic.

"What is he saying?' Dan whispered to Diana.

"He is telling them not to listen to us—to leave," she said quietly.

The priest shouted again, and the people shifted nervously in their seats. They cast anxious glances at each other.

With a sharp movement, the unfamiliar man stood up. He strode over to the priest, his jaw set, and grabbed the drunken man by the arms. The priest struggled fruitlessly as the man turned him around and marched him out of the assembly. With a light push, the man sent the priest back down the road from where he had come.

Everyone, including the team, stared at him wonderingly. The man walked back towards the crowd, disregarding their awed gazes.

"Don't have anything to do with that man," he said firmly, sweeping his eyes over the congregation. "He does not have love."

He looked up at the team, and nodded his head briefly. "You have love." He went back to his seat and sat down, waiting for the service to continue.

Dan stared at the man for a moment longer and then shook himself.

"Uh...would you finish sharing?" he asked his teammate, gesturing for her to step back up to the front.

A little awkwardly, she resumed her testimony. Throughout the rest of the service, everyone kept sneaking glances at the man. He just sat quietly, looking straight ahead at the team, listening intently. When the team shared the gospel, the man was one of those who raised their hands to accept Christ as Savior.

After the service wrapped up, Dan went down and found the man. They introduced themselves, and Dan found out he was a Druze—a small religious sect and a very unreached people group. The man invited Dan and the team to come to his house the next day. There, the team had the privilege of sharing the gospel with the man's wife and his seven sons. The entire family accepted Christ as their Savior.

A new house church was started in the man's home, and in that week 121 people professed faith in Christ. God had moved mightily. He had used a broken, rag-tag team of people, and Dan, who was leading his first team to Israel and who had felt completely clueless about how to share the gospel with so many different peoples.

Dan remembered how the apostle Paul had said in Romans 1:16-17, "For I am not ashamed of the gospel of Christ, for it is the power of God to salvation for everyone who believes, for the Jew first and also for the Greek. For in it the righteousness of God is revealed from faith to faith; as it is written, 'The just shall live by faith.'" Because they had stepped out in faith and surrendered to His power, God had moved in their ministry—and He had worked His wonders.

It's a Miracle

A short time after his team returned to America, Dan received word from Israel. The youngest son of the Druze family who had come to Jesus was terribly sick. His name was Abraham, and he was 18 years old. Abraham had cancer all throughout his body, and the doctors were saying he only had a few days to live. The family's community had shunned them. "This is the curse of God on your family for changing your religion," they cried. They wouldn't have anything to do with them. But the Christians believed God could heal Abraham. They called for prayer.

Dan began to pray fervently for Abraham and his family, and he shared the request with as many believers as he could. Abraham was on the hearts of many, many people, all praying desperately for God, if He so chose, to heal Abraham for His glory.

Then, supernaturally, the cancer was gone. The doctors were helpless to provide an explanation. No one could understand it—no one except the believers, who praised God for the miracle and rejoiced with Abraham's family as they welcomed their son back home.

Dan heard the story, thrilled. He remembered when the family had first accepted Christ. Already they had faced a terrible trial, but they had continued to trust God. There were strong believers rising up in the Holy Land, and God was doing amazing things there.

In response to the continued work, Dan prepared to lead another team to Israel. Their connections had strengthened during the last trip, and now they were ready to mount a full-scale ministry outreach. Instead of 11 people, this team was composed of 49 short-term missionaries. They would be working in five different locations across Israel—including Jerusalem, Nazareth, and Canaan—and would be sharing the gospel among five different people groups.

"Dan, there's all this amazing stuff going on," Kurt, one of the e3 Partners staff, said eagerly. "You should get a videographer to capture it."

Dan rubbed his forehead wearily. "I have 49 people I need to keep track of," he said. "I'm making plans involving five different hotels and 17 mini-vans. I'm dealing with a government that doesn't want us to come and work in their country." He grinned wryly. "I barely have enough time to finish everything else I need to do—so if you want a videographer, you're going to have to find one."

Before Dan's team left for Israel, Kurt approached Dan again.

"I've found you a videographer," he said.

Dan looked at him, slightly surprised. "Oh—thank you."

Kurt smiled, handing him a paper with the videographer's information. "He and his wife will meet you in Nazareth."

After a long plane ride, Dan and his team of 49 people landed in Israel. They all gathered in Nazareth before traveling to their separate locations across the country. There, the videographer met Dan.

The videographer was a strongly-built, solemn-faced young man, with distinctly Arab features. He shook Dan's hand firmly. "My name is Jamal," he said, "and this is my wife, Latifa." He motioned for his wife, a beautiful young woman, to step up beside him.

Dan smiled at Latifa in greeting. "How long have you been married?"

Jamal grinned. "Seventeen days."

They were newlyweds. Dan's smile broadened. "Well, congratulations to both of you," he said warmly.

"What is the plan for the videos?" Jamal asked.

Dan had been considering this on the flight over, and he knew just the place to start. "First we're going to go up to Mt. Carmel, to Isofia. There's a family there I'd like to interview."

The next day Jamal and Latifa packed up their video equipment, and Dan drove them all up to Abraham's house. He had spoken with the family about the interview. They were delighted and eager to share about what they had experienced.

At the house, Dan reunited with the family and introduced Jamal and Latifa.

"I'll be interviewing you," Dan explained to the family, "And Jamal will be recording with his camera. Jamal," Dan said, turning to him. "Do you want to set them up how you need them?"

Jamal nodded. "Please, come this way," he said to the family. He seated Abraham and his mother on a couch and had the father stand behind. Dan sat just to the left of them to ask the questions. Jamal set up his camera and checked the framing, while Latifa positioned the video-light and held it steady.

There was a moment of quiet adjustments and whispers, and then Jamal signaled that Dan could begin.

"So—can you tell us a little about yourselves and your testimony?" Dan asked.

Taking turns, the family described how they had once been Druze, but, a year ago, had come to know Jesus when Dan had shared the gospel with them.

"Everything has changed," the father said. "When the believers came to our town, we saw the love and joy that they had. Now, because of Jesus, we know it too."

"A church was started in our home," the mother said. "Fellow believers came and worshipped with us, and studied the Bible."

"And what happened shortly after that?" Dan asked.

"The doctors said I had cancer," Abraham spoke out. "They said I wasn't going to live much longer."

Out of the corner of his eye, Dan saw Jamal look up from the camera.

"The community said it was God's curse on our family," the mother said in a low voice, tears in her eyes. "But I knew—I knew God could heal my son."

"Many people prayed for me," Abraham went on. "And then—the cancer was gone. All of it. The doctors were shocked, everyone was shocked. No one could explain what had happened."

Jamal had forgotten about the camera. Trembling slightly, he turned towards Dan. "It's a miracle," he whispered, "isn't it?"

Dan looked at Jamal, and nodded slowly. "Yeah, Jamal," he said softly. "It's a miracle."

Crash! Everyone jumped, startled, as the video-light fell sideways, throwing a weird, leaping glow over the room. Jamal leapt to his feet, Dan right beside him.

"Latifa?" Jamal cried. He jumped over the fallen light and knelt down beside his wife. She was lying crumpled beside the couch, passed out.

Dan stood back, his pulse racing from the rush of adrenaline, as Abraham's mother went to Latifa's side. The video light lay on the floor, painting a large golden circle on the ceiling.

"Here, let's lift her onto the couch," the mother said. Jamal scooped Latifa up and laid her on the cushions, his brow creased with worry. They made sure she was cool, and Abraham ran and got her a cup of water.

Gradually, Latifa came around. Her eyelids fluttered, and she groaned and began trying to sit up.

"Lie back," Jamal said gently. "Are you alright?"

Latifa nodded. "I—I've only passed out like that once before," she said, putting a hand to her head. "When..." She swallowed hard, her eyes growing haunted as she remembered. "When Saddam Hussein had those people killed in Baghdad for hoarding food." She closed her eyes briefly as if to shut out the memory. "But it's never happened since then—not until now."

She looked up at Abraham's mother, tears shining in her eyes. "Your story is truly amazing, how your son—" she broke off and turned to Jamal, who gave her a small smile.

"It is a miracle," he said.

"Yes," Latifa whispered. "A miracle."

"Words are inadequate to express all the benefits of participating with e3 Partners on an expedition. They prepare and equip you. Then, you get to evangelize with local church leaders. Finally, the efforts are used to establish the local churches producing lasting results. If you want an adventure, join an e3 expedition!"

Dr. Ken Lang, Pastor
Calvary Chapel of Syracuse, NY

Caught on Camera

So began Jamal and Latifa's journey with the team. Dan and his friend, Craig, drove all across the country with Jamal and Latifa to video the outreach going on in different locations. They traveled from Haifa to Nazareth and from Canaan to Ariel, where a team was working with Victor Bloom to reach Russian Jews. Everywhere they went, Jamal and Latifa recorded what they saw.

The couple captured how the gospel was shared from house-to-house, how many people heard and accepted—and how pure, radiant joy came into the faces of the new believers as they claimed Christ as their Savior. Jamal and Latifa videoed worship services where the 49 Americans praised God with their Israeli family. They videoed prayer times and Bible studies, and while they did their job, they heard the truth of God. They heard the gospel over and over again, but more importantly, they saw true Christianity being lived out by these missionaries.

Previously, Jamal and Latifa had done videos and interviews for televangelists: people who really just wanted fame and wealth in exchange for their preaching. This had been the only encounter Jamal and Latifa had had with Christianity—until now. Now they saw what God's message was truly about: sacrificing yourself, sharing the Good News, loving people, helping people, and showing them how to have joy and hope through Jesus.

"So," Jamal asked from the back seat, as Craig drove towards their next location, "What do you do—in Christianity—if someone gets drunk?"

Dan twisted around in the front passenger seat to look back at Jamal. "Well," he said, making sure he had his thoughts together, "We sober them up, and then show them the Scriptures where it says, 'Do not be drunk with wine, but be filled with the Holy Spirit.' And then we tell them about living a godly life, one that glorifies God, and how being drunk dishonors His Name."

"What if they get drunk again?" Jamal asked.

Dan hesitated. "Well...about the same thing. Maybe we say it a bit stronger, more tough love, you know, but...about the same thing."

"In Islam," Jamal said stoically, "We beat them the first time. The second time, we kill them."

Dan nodded slowly. "You see, we believe that we are to love one another just as Christ loved us," he explained, "And He loved us while we were still sinners."

Jamal fell silent, his brows narrowed in deep thought. For a moment Dan watched Jamal staring out the window at the passing landscape. *Lord, please help him understand Your truth,* Dan prayed.

As their journey continued, Dan and Craig found out more and more about Jamal and Latifa. The couple began to open up during the long days and nights that their little team spent together. One day, Jamal showed Dan a bullet-hole in his leg.

"Latifa's brother didn't like me," Jamal said, looking down at the ugly scar. "When I was courting her, he shot me, and filled my car with bullets."

A short while afterwards, Dan found out that Latifa's uncle had been one of the most wanted terrorists in the world. And Jamal had trained in weapons in 13 different countries, could field dress a bazooka and drive a tank—all trademarks of a Hamas terrorist.

This isn't just your average couple, Dan thought nervously. That night, as they drove across Israel with Jamal and Latifa sitting quietly in the backseat, Dan began to worry. Jamal's background gave him every reason to hate Christians. Here they were, alone and in the middle of nowhere. If Jamal wanted to, he could easily kill him and Craig both. He certainly had the training.

But every day, with the same composed, solemn air, Jamal followed Dan and Craig wherever they went. Never once did he show any signs of hostility. He asked them questions during the long drives, about Jesus and about what they believed. He and Latifa videoed the team's ministry, and with every day, they saw and learned more and more.

After an amazing, hectic week of traveling and ministry and evangelism, the team's time in Israel was drawing to a close. A few of the Americans had already headed home, but the rest gathered in Nazareth, where they would start a week-long tour of the Holy Land. In Nazareth, Dan met with Jamal and Latifa, to thank them and to say goodbye.

"Dan, I was wondering..." Jamal asked, "Your tour will end in Jerusalem—that's where I live. I have nine friends, Hamas seekers, who want to know God just like I do. When you come to Jerusalem, would you speak with them and tell them what you told me?"

Dan felt a slight chill run through him. Nine other Hamas seekers? And Jamal was asking him to meet with them—alone? It could very, very easily be a trap. Jamal had almost been killed, just because his girlfriend's family didn't care for him. If he, a Muslim, could be attacked in that way, how much more likely would it be for a Christian to be murdered?

Dan looked at Jamal. Jamal still maintained his solemn, composed air, but there was a light, an eagerness in his eyes as he awaited Dan's answer. Dan hated to think that Jamal would try to kill him.

"Will you come?" Jamal asked, pleadingly.

Lord, give me wisdom, Dan prayed. He was scared—yes, he was. But he took a deep breath and said, "Sure, I'll come."

Jamal broke into a smile. "Thank you!" He pulled out his phone and soon was talking animatedly to someone on the other line. "Hey, I've got this friend from America who's coming to Jerusalem. He can tell us some things—would you be there?"

Dan hung back, his thoughts whirling. What had he just agreed to do?

I See Love

After the gathering at Nazareth, Jamal and Latifa left for Jerusalem, and Dan and the others went off on their tour of Israel. They visited all the famous sites and cities, like Masada, Jericho, the Sea of Galilee, Bethlehem, and Samaria. The tour was amazing, but all the while the meeting with Jamal was pressing on the back of Dan's mind. He had told the rest of the team about it, and he knew they were all in prayer. But he was still anxious.

At the end of the week, for the last stop of their tour, the team arrived in Jerusalem. Dan knew this was his last chance to back out of the arrangement. Again he prayed for wisdom, and the whole team prayed with him.

Afterwards, Dan called Jamal's cell phone.

"I'm here," Dan said. "I'm ready to see your friends."

Jamal thanked Dan again and gave him the address of the meeting place. Then Dan said goodbye to the team.

"We'll all be praying for you," his friend Craig said anxiously.

"Thank you," Dan replied.

Dan left the hotel alone. Outside, he hailed a taxi, and told the driver the address that Jamal had given him. Nodding, the driver pulled out into the road.

As the car drove through the streets of Jerusalem, Dan sat in silence, trying to remember the method for sharing the gospel with Muslims. He wasn't fresh on the statutes of Islam, and he couldn't quite remember how to bridge to the Bible through the Quran...he had been studying witnessing to Jews before he left the States. *What am I going to say to these Hamas seekers?* he thought.

Dan's stomach gave a queasy lurch as the taxi braked and came to a stop. Quickly, he glanced out the window. The taxi had parked right outside an open-air dining area. Dan let out a small sigh of relief. The meeting place was public, which made him feel a bit better.

Dan paid the taxi driver and climbed out onto the street, casting his eyes around for Jamal.

"Dan!"

Dan heard the shout from a short distance off. Jamal waved enthusiastically at him, Latifa at his side. The couple was standing next to a table, which had a small group gathered around it.

Here we go, Dan thought as he walked up to meet them.

"Everyone's here," Jamal said, stepping forward to greet Dan. "They're ready to hear what you say."

"Jamal," Dan said suddenly, "What exactly do you want me to talk about?"

"Just what you told me," Jamal said easily, "About loving others, about what Jesus taught, about the Bible. We are all still new believers—we have much to learn."

Dan stared at Jamal, something clicking in his mind. "You're...all new believers?"

Jamal nodded, a smile beginning to spread across his face. "I became convinced of who Jesus was after spending time with you and the missionaries and learning about your faith. I accepted Christ as my Savior. Then Latifa and I told our friends, and they too accepted Christ. I was hoping you would follow-up with them."

Dan could barely keep back a laugh of joy and relief. "Jamal! I would love to!"

Grinning, Jamal led Dan to the table where his nine friends were waiting. Dan greeted all of them and spent the rest of the time answering all of their questions as best as he could. As he looked around at the 11 new believers, all Dan could do was praise God. *Thank you, Jesus, for reaching Jamal and Latifa, and for putting the desire in their hearts to share You with others.*

For these 11 believers, however, their faith had not come without a cost. When Dan spoke with Jamal after the meeting, he found out that Jamal's father had separated him and Latifa, and had published an ad in the newspaper formally disowning him. Jamal's uncle had fired him from his job. Jamal's brother had wanted to kill him—but his father, still loving his son and hoping that Jamal would turn back to Islam, had not allowed it. And Jamal's friend, Mahmoud, one of the new believers, had had his car firebombed. Dan was shaken as he realized that all this had happened within five days—five days from the time Jamal and Latifa had arrived back in Jerusalem to when Dan and the team had gotten there at the end of their tour. Already, these new believers had suffered much for their Lord.

Before the team left for America, they held one last celebration service to wrap up the trip. Dan asked if Jamal would come speak to the team. He agreed.

"Jamal," Dan asked him, when they stood before the team at the service, "Why did you come to Christ?"

Jamal turned to look at the crowd of missionaries. "In Islam," he said, "All I see are mothers weeping for their children." He paused, and he fixed the team with his serious, steady gaze. "In Christianity—in you—I see love. It was Christ's love that brought me to Him."

Two Fish

Vern was a very orderly man. He was an engineer, and he had an engineer's mind set; he liked things to be plain, clear, and logical. He was not easily frightened. In fact, his daughter Lorie had never seen him afraid of anything.

Today, however, Vern was scared. He was in Haifa, Israel, with his daughter Lorie on a trip to share the gospel. But Vern had never shared his faith before. He wasn't sure how to tell someone else about the gospel.

"Just follow the EvangeCube, Dad," Lorie said gently. She and Vern were about to go out as a team for their first day of ministry.

Vern tried to sound confident. "Alright then, let's go," he said.

Lorie and her father left the house, and shortly afterwards, out in town, they met a man named Abu Nami. He was an Arab father—Abu meaning father, and Nami referring to his first-born son. Lorie started a conversation with him while Vern hung in the background, nervously knitting his fingers together.

The man seemed friendly enough. He engaged heartily in the discussion, and when Lorie brought up Jesus he was open and willing to listen. It happened so smoothly, so naturally. Lorie moved into the gospel message, telling Abu Nami about how Jesus came to earth to die

19

for sinners.

Vern watched in awe as the old man took Lorie's hands and tearfully said, "I want to know Jesus. How can I do it?"

Lorie bowed her head with him, and Abu Nami prayed for Jesus to take away his sins and be his Lord and Savior. Vern's legs were trembling. He stared at his daughter, burning tears filling his eyes. Sniffing, he blinked and let them course down his cheeks. His Lorie had just brought someone to Christ. She had shared her faith, and this Arab man had been saved! Vern could hardly believe it. He knew that he wanted desperately to understand the joy Lorie had had on her face as she told Abu Nami about Jesus.

The first time Vern worked up the courage to share his own faith, his mouth was dry and his hands could barely open the cube. Stuttering slightly, Vern moved through each panel and explained the pictures. When Vern raised his head, the person with whom he was sharing was crying. The young man asked Vern to pray with him. Vern was shocked. Feeling completely inadequate, Vern knelt beside the young man and held his hands as he prayed to receive Christ.

While the young man prayed, Vern felt a powerful joy beginning to swell deep within him. God was using him, Vern, to bring another soul to salvation. Despite his fear and his hesitancy, God had spoken through him. Vern continued to share the gospel during the week-long mission trip in Israel, and each time someone came to Christ he felt a fresh surge of disbelief and amazement—and joy.

After a week had passed, the team took some time off from ministry and went on a tour of Israel. When Lorie had first proposed the trip to Vern, this tour was really why he had agreed to go. But now he had experienced firsthand the amazing experience that evangelism was, and, though seeing the sights was spectacular, the memories that Vern held to most fondly were the conversations from the week before.

On the last day of their trip, the team stayed in a hotel on the Sea of Galilee. Vern rose early that morning. He took his Bible out onto the porch where he could see the sun breaking in soft, rosy splendor over the placid waters of the sea, wreathing the horizon in golden mist. The air was cool and sharp with salt.

Sighing in contentment, Vern settled down to have his quiet time. But then as he glanced out at the docks, he saw the silhouette of a lone man fishing by the Sea of Galilee. He didn't have a pole, just a line that he let hang down into the water.

Vern watched the fisherman for a moment. Then he leapt to his feet and ran into the hotel.

Lorie heard footsteps pounding down the hallway outside of her and Dan's hotel room. Suddenly someone was knocking frantically on the door. Lorie hurried to answer, worried that something was wrong. When she opened the door, her father stood outside, panting.

"Do you have another EvangeCube?" he gasped. "I gave my last one away."

Bewildered, Lorie pulled one out of her bag and handed it to him. "But why do you need..."

"Thank you!" Vern said, cutting her off excitedly. He dashed back down the hallway and disappeared around a corner, leaving Lorie staring after him.

Vern ran outside and down the dock to where the fisherman was sitting. The man glanced up as Vern approached. He was a Ukrainian.

"Hello," Vern said, gulping to get his breath back. "Do you mind if I join you?"

The man smiled pleasantly. "No, not at all," he said in a thickly accented voice. Vern sat down next to him and swung his feet over the edge of the dock.

Before long, the two men were talking amiably. The Ukrainian introduced himself as Sergei. He offered Vern a fishing line, and after a few minutes, Vern managed to haul a sizable fish up onto the dock. Sergei slapped Vern on the back. "Well done!" he exclaimed.

Vern grinned proudly. They tossed the fish back into the shimmering water and continued chatting. Then, so smoothly, so naturally, Vern saw an opportunity to share the gospel. He felt the now familiar guidance of the Holy Spirit, and, using the cube, he talked to Sergei about God, Jesus, and salvation. Sergei listened with full attention to the gospel message; his face seemed strained with longing.

"Would you like to accept Jesus?" Vern asked.

Sergei nodded vigorously. "Yes. I need Him to save me. I want to know Him." He paused, his brow wrinkled in thought. "But I want to ask Him in my own tongue," he said at last. "In Russian."

Vern smiled. "Yes. Yes, of course."

Sergei got down on his knees on the sun-drenched dock, and there, as the waves lapped the shores of the Sea of Galilee, the Ukrainian man prayed in Russian for Jesus to be his Savior.

Vern knew now that sharing the gospel wasn't just for an official evangelism trip. It was for anytime the Lord put someone in your path that needed to hear about His love and salvation. As Jesus had said, His followers are to be fishers of men. And that day, Vern caught two fish—one from the sea, and one for the Kingdom.

To India by Faith

While Dan was working at the e3 Partners' Dallas office, the church he attended asked him to serve as chairman of their missions committee. After a time of prayer, Dan accepted the position.

Dan rifled through a stack of reports which had come in from the various missionaries that the church supported. One was from a national Indian missionary named Peter Kashung. Peter had a tremendous passion and vision to plant churches in his home country of India. Immediately upon reading his story, Dan's interest was sparked. E3 partners, the organization Dan was a part of, worked with people just like Peter—helping nationals to plant churches in their own countries.

Dan checked the differing time zones and when it was a reasonable hour in India, he dialed Peter's number. "Hello," Dan said when Peter answered the phone, "My name is Dan Hitzhusen, and I'm the chairman of Dallas Bible Church's missions committee. I read about your work in India. I work with e3 Partners. We partner with local missionaries to help them plant churches. Is there any way we could help you in your ministry?"

"Wow, that would be amazing," Peter said, his voice sounding relieved. "I've heard about the good work of e3 Partners. Would you be able to come to India? We've been asking for help for many years, but no one has ever come."

"I'll see what we can do," Dan assured him. The two said goodbye, and Dan went off to research the area where Peter lived and see what would have to be done to bring a team there.

The part of India where Peter lived was called Manipur. It was a province of India torn by warring factions and tribes. It had also been closed to foreigners for 50 years, and the only way to get in was to get special restricted area permits. Dan leaned back in his chair, troubled. He felt strongly that they should go help Peter, but it looked like getting there would be more of a challenge than he had anticipated.

The trip began to come together when Dallas Bible Church offered to partner with Dan. The church raised up a team to accompany him to India, and Peter assured Dan that he would acquire the restricted area permits.

During the process of planning the trip, Dan attended a meeting with Patrick Johnstone, a renowned Christian researcher. As they talked, Dan told Patrick about the upcoming trip to Manipur.

"Dan, you will never get into Manipur," Patrick said seriously. "It's completely closed off. You *can't* get in."

Dan hesitated, struggling with how to respond. "Thank you, Patrick," he said at last. "I appreciate you telling me."

Now Dan was unsure of what to do. This was a man whom he respected and trusted. If he said that getting into Manipur was impossible, shouldn't Dan listen? But Dan still felt that God was leading them on this trip and that, somehow, they were supposed to go.

The next Sunday at church, one of the women who was on the missionary team approached Dan.

"I've been talking to three of my friends," she said haltingly. "They used to be war correspondents. And...well, they said they wouldn't be caught dead in northeast India. They said no one should go there. It's too dangerous." She looked up at Dan, her eyes scared.

Dan opened his mouth to respond, but what could he say? It was true that Manipur was dangerous. But that didn't necessarily mean that they shouldn't go.

The church leadership prayed. After deciding that it was too dangerous to send anyone to Manipur, the church pulled their team out of the mission trip.

Now what? Dan had no missionary team, no permits, and if anyone was going to go help Peter, Dan had to buy the airline tickets very soon. But what was the point of buying tickets if there was no team to use them?

Dan lay in his bed, wide awake. He couldn't get India off his mind. He kept remembering Peter and the relief in his voice when Dan told him they would come and help. He thought of Manipur and the tribes who lived there and the people who were lost and had no church in their village. Dan sighed heavily. What was he to do? Finally he forced his eyes closed, and, after several restless minutes, he fell asleep.

With a gasp of shock, Dan awoke. His eyes were wide open and he was soaked with sweat. Dan struggled to sit up, but his arms and legs were pinned down. He couldn't move; he couldn't even lift his hand. A horrible terror spread over him, like a chill running down his back. He felt something evil in the room. It pressed down on him, paralyzing his body, raising goose-bumps on his skin. Dan sucked in a quick breath, trying to find his voice through the panic that gripped him. "In the Name of Jesus and His shed blood on the cross," he shouted hoarsely, "You have no power over me. Leave this place!"

Instantly, Dan felt the pressure release. He breathed in sharply, sitting up and swinging his legs over the edge of the bed. For a long moment he just sat there. His clothes were cold and damp, and his whole body was trembling. The fear lingered at the back of his mind like a foul taste in his mouth.

Dan got up and knelt to pray. "Thank You, Jesus, for Your power over the evil one," he prayed. He took in a deep breath, feeling his tension ease. "Thank You for Your peace."

As Dan got back in bed, one thing was clear to him—the enemy did not want a team to go to India. So Dan became even more certain that God did.

Back in San Diego, a church called New Hope Church had supported Dan and Lorie for some time. The pastor there, Joe, had officiated at their wedding, and the church had backed them when they decided to join e3 Partners. After the fearful attack in the night, Dan received word that Joe's church had ten people who could go with Dan to Manipur. They were mostly housewives; of the men there were two engineers, one who was legally blind. Only two people out of the whole team had ever been on a mission trip before. But they were willing.

Dan could see that God was providing. They still didn't have their restricted area permits, but in faith, Dan paid $10,000—non-refundable—for the airplane tickets to Manipur.

Two months passed. The day came for the team to leave for India and their permits still hadn't been confirmed. But Dan and the team continued to trust that this trip was God's plan.

Although they had faith that they were following God's direction, the whole team was a little anxious. What if they arrived without the permits? Would they have crossed the ocean for nothing? And then what if they did make it into Manipur? What would await them there? They had heard about the danger they would be heading into. The prospect of serving in Manipur scared many of them, though they had still agreed to go.

One of the men, the legally blind engineer named Dan W., was rethinking that decision.

On the way to the airport he couldn't stop shaking and sweating, knowing that the moment he got on that plane he wouldn't be able to turn back. When Dan stopped the car for gas, Dan W. couldn't contain himself any longer.

Dan climbed back into the car and checked to be sure that everyone was there. "Hey. Where's Dan W.?" he asked, frowning.

The other passengers looked around. "I don't know," one of the women said.

"Wait, I think I see him!" The other engineer exclaimed, pointing out the window.

Dan narrowed his eyes to peer through the gathering twilight. He saw the faint outline of a person some distance off—it was the engineer, trying to run away. Dan asked God for a special allowance of mercy and jogged off after the fugitive.

A few moments later Dan caught up, and he managed to talk the engineer into returning to the car. Then Dan shut the doors and continued driving to the airport.

The team arrived, checked their luggage, and found their gate. Still no permits. They boarded the flight, and the plane took off right on schedule. Still no permits. They were on their way now...

When the team landed in Singapore, their last stop before India, Dan got word that their permits had been issued. With exclamations of praise and relief, the team thanked God for overcoming another obstacle in their mission.

The plane landed in Manipur, where the Indian Army with their AK-47s was guarding the airport. The permits were there. And fortunately, so were Peter Kashung and his family. Their children had brought leis of flowers which they draped over the American's necks, giggling shyly. The team began to smile more freely; the feeling of tension and fear relaxed. Peter and his wife Moala welcomed them enthusiastically and drove them all to their hotel where they could begin settling in.

Once the team had set their luggage down, Peter turned to face them. "We are so glad you're here," he said seriously. "We will be sending you to our four toughest villages."

Dan wished he could give Peter a proverbial kick under the table. He had hoped to mentally and spiritually prepare his team for whatever Peter might ask. Now the men and women were looking at Dan with anxious expressions as though expecting him to take charge and let Peter know what they weren't capable of doing.

"One village produces all the drugs and wine for this region," Peter continued. "One village is completely communist. The other is a well-known terrorist center. And in the last village you'll be going to, thirteen of my evangelists were beaten and one almost killed last week."

The team stared at Peter. He smiled, seeming not to notice the color that had drained from their faces. "Thank you so much for coming to help us."

Dan cleared his throat. "Peter, my team and I should probably go check into our rooms. We've been traveling for 48 hours now, and..." as Dan glanced at his team, "I think we'll need to regroup with a time of prayer and then get some rest."

If you have an iPhone, iPad or Mac computer,
go to your iBooks Store and
download *Cat and Dog Behaviors, Vol. 1-5*.
Each book has over 120 videos
of Cats with rude behavior
and Dogs with good behavior.

It's a great parenting tool based on the cartoon book,
102 Differences Between Cats and Dogs for Kids.

The Terrorist Village

Dan and the team had a few days to pray and think about what they were going to do. Before beginning outreach to these villages in India, the team would be participating in a huge celebration hosted by Peter's tribe—the Nagas. The team had arrived at the 100th anniversary of the gospel coming to the Naga tribe. The Nagas used to be a head-hunting tribe. In fact, Peter's father had been a fierce warrior with over 150 heads in his collection. But then, 100 years ago, an American named William Pettigrew had come to their village and led five Nagas to Christ. From there the gospel had spread, until 90 percent of the Naga tribe were Christians. Now the Nagas honored the American missionary team in memory of the time when another American had brought them the gospel.

Every night, the team visited a different church in the area. Before they entered the building, the Nagas would lay out a red carpet leading up to the church and set out high-backed chairs for all the Americans. Then the Nagas would perform beautiful dances for them, twirling and trailing their many colors through the air. It was a magnificent sight. When it came time to go up to the church, the Nagas would gather in throngs along the sides of the road, cheering the team on as they walked past. When the team entered the building, it was packed with people who had gathered to hear the Americans speak.

Those evenings, so full of rejoicing and praise, encouraged the team. But when they came back to their hotel, the graveness of their situation weighed heavily on them again. The Nagas themselves were afraid to share the gospel with the Meiteis and were praying fervently for the team's safety. The whole team spent those few days in earnest prayer, especially Dan. He prayed for wisdom. As team leader, he did not want to make a wrong decision and potentially send his team to their deaths.

"Each of you will have to make the choice for yourself," Dan told them one night. "Pray and talk with your families. The danger will be very real. You need to decide, between you and God, what you should do."

They nodded soberly. Now that they were here, the conflict of the area was clearly visible. The Naga tribe and another Christian tribe were in continual warfare with the Meiteis, a fierce snake-worshiping tribe who opposed the Christians. At the same time, the Indian government, with its soldiers and machine guns, was fighting against the national rebels who were trying to overthrow the government. There was constant chaos from bombs, attacks, and skirmishes—and a great deal of crossfire from multiple factions.

After lengthy discussion and prayer, the team decided to go ahead with the mission. They were still afraid, but they trusted that this was what they were supposed to do.

The next morning, the Americans prepared to team up with their national partners and interpreters to begin ministry in the villages. Dan and Tricia (the wife of Dan's home church's pastor) had agreed to take the terrorist village. Both of them, after much prayer, had felt the Lord leading them there.

The team split up and headed out to the four Meitei villages. A jeep took Dan and Tricia to a home on the outskirts of the village where they would be working. They met up with their local team of nationals and interpreters, prayed together, and from there, the whole group walked up the street and into the village.

Once they had a gone a little way, Dan's interpreter stopped. "Alright, here is where we split up," he said. "But remember—don't go out of sight." Dan and Tricia nodded. The two broke up, gathering with their interpreters, and went off down each side of the road.

For a few minutes they didn't see anyone. Then Dan turned a corner. Suddenly ten young men came walking rapidly towards him. They were all in their twenties and were led by a strong, formidable-looking young man who strode towards the newcomers with a determined glare.

Dan watched uneasily as the men surrounded him and his interpreter, their stances aggressive. Their leader walked straight up to Dan. Dan stood his ground, staring into the other man's eyes. The young Indian was barely three inches from his face.

What's going to happen? Dan thought. His heartbeat quickened though he tried to remain calm.

"I want to know this Jesus," the man said earnestly.

Dan looked at him blankly. *Really?* In his astonishment, it was all he could think.

"Well...I'm glad," Dan said, hoping he sounded as confident as if he had been expecting that question all along. He looked around at the men on every side and at his nervous interpreter huddled next to him. "Let me tell you how you can know Jesus."

Dan shared the gospel with the entire group of men, and five of them asked to receive Jesus as their Savior. The leader's name was Nilikaanta. When Dan offered to lead him in prayer, Nilikaanta bowed his head.

Afterwards, Dan gave Nilikaanta a short form to fill out. The team used the forms to know what decision each person had made, so that the nationals could do follow-up. But when Nilikaanta went over the paper, he didn't check that he had accepted Christ. Dan noticed.

"We'll be back tomorrow," Dan told him. "Can we meet with you and talk more?"

Nilikaanta agreed.

That night, Dan and Tricia returned to the Naga tribe, praising God for what He had already accomplished in the Meitei village. Each of the returning teams had also experienced God's power and protection in their various locations.

All of the teams attended a Naga church service together, where they spoke and shared with the people there. As Dan finished speaking, a woman stepped out of the crowd.

"Don't be afraid," she said boldly. "I had a vision last night. I saw angels surrounding you wherever you go."

Dan and the team felt their anxiety subsiding. Not only had things gone well on the first day, but the message this vision seemed to give was comforting—they would be safe.

No Matter What the Cost

The next day, as before, Dan and Tricia traveled to the Meitei village, where their national partners were waiting. They entered the house, ready to begin another day sharing the gospel. They were eager to see what God had planned.

But when they came inside, the faces which greeted them were grim.

"What's wrong?" Tricia asked, concerned.

Dan's interpreter stepped forward, shaken and pale. "I had a dream last night," he said. "Something terrible is going to happen!"

Dan and Tricia looked at each other. What did this mean? Hadn't the woman's vision spoken of protection?

The interpreter fell to his knees, blocking the doorway leading outside. "Please don't go into the village!" he cried, his eyes wide with panic. "Please!"

"We believe God wants us to work here," Dan said slowly.

The man seized Dan's hands desperately. "Please, no," he begged. Tears slipped from his eyes. "Father God, please…" he began praying. "Take my life if you must…please, spare them! Please…"

Dan knelt beside him, putting a hand on his shoulder. "Let's all ask God what we should

29

do," he said quietly.

The whole team huddled together and prayed fervently for wisdom. Each one asked God to direct their decision. Afterwards, they talked together and discussed what should be done.

In response to the leading of the Holy Spirit, everyone agreed that the ministry should continue.

"We'll be careful," Dan said. "How about let's leapfrog the houses that we visit so that we can stay within close range of each other."

The team nodded. Dan's interpreter, still trembling, finally nodded his head in affirmation as well.

"Let's step out in faith and in the power of God," Dan said, "and see what He's going to do."

The team separated into their groups and moved into the village, keeping each other in view at all times. For the whole morning, they shared the gospel house-to-house and witnessed several people respond to the message.

It was almost noontime, as they were walking up the street towards the next house, when they heard a sudden pulse of sound coming from the town center. A sharp, resonating boom—like an explosion.

The team glanced towards each other and started hurrying to the town square.

A crowd of over 400 people were milling around the courtyard of the Hindu temple, staring numbly at each other or talking intensely to their neighbors. Some had been near the scene, but most rushed to the spot after hearing what had happened. A short distance off, the remnants of a small building lay in a crumbled heap. Someone had set off a bomb, and several people had been killed.

Dan and Tricia and the nationals stood at the edge of the courtyard, wondering what to do. All these people were gathered, in the midst of this tragedy, needing to hear a message of hope. How could they reach out to them?

Again, their whole team gathered together in prayer. They asked God to show them how to tell the people of His love.

"What would be the best way to share with them?" Dan asked the nationals.

They talked together for a while, and then one of them suggested, "What if we ask the gospel band to play?"

Someone ran and got a group of locals who had formed an Indian gospel band. They brought out all their instruments and set up right in the middle of the courtyard in front of a big Hindu god. Then they began to play. Their songs about Jesus were lively and soulful, sung in the local Meitei dialect. The crowd began listening.

By the time the band finished playing, they had everyone's attention. So when the team came up after them, the people were prepared to listen.

"No one can know when they are going to die," a national began. Solemnly, he gestured to the pile of rubble. "This tragedy reminds all of us of that."

"That is why it is so important to know what will happen to you after you die," Tricia said. She told the people about the one true God, who loved them so much that He had sent two people all the way from America to tell them the Good News.

Then Dan shared the gospel with the crowd gathered at the Hindu temple. He told them how everyone can know the God of the universe—the God who loves them. At the end of the presentation, half of the 450 people raised their hands to accept Christ as their Savior.

The tragedy of the bombing caused a bigger outreach opportunity than the team could have imagined. They realized that both visions had been true. Something terrible had happened in the village that day. But God had also protected them. And as they trusted His will and stepped out in faith, He had led them on the right path.

At last Dan nudged Tricia, pointing to his watch. "It's time to meet Nilikaanta," he said.

Nilikaanta was waiting when Dan and Tricia arrived at the prearranged meeting place.

"When we gave you the form yesterday," Dan asked him, "why did you not say that you accepted Jesus as your Savior?"

The man evaded Dan's eyes for a moment, and then he began to speak. "If I say yes to Jesus," he said, "My family will kick me out, and I will have no place to go. I will lose my job. Most likely, the villagers will beat me."

Dan was suddenly at a loss for words. What could he say to Nilikaanta? As an American, he didn't have to risk everything on a daily basis to worship Jesus. Dan prayed for guidance. He had no idea how to relate to what this man was going through.

"I have never had to face this kind of persecution," Dan said haltingly. "I really can't understand your situation or help you make this choice with advice. But...I know I serve a God who has been persecuted. And I know that He is worth suffering for."

Nilikaanta listened, his eyes shining. Dan and Tricia went through many different passages: intense, difficult scriptures that dealt with persecution. The Holy Spirit led them to simply share with Nilikaanta the truth of God's Word, not try to speak any of their own words. This was between Nilikaanta and God.

Tricia told Nilikaanta the stories of Paul, who had been beaten, stoned, shipwrecked, and imprisoned, and of Jesus, who had been ridiculed and whipped beyond recognition.

"The Bible says that we are not to fear the one who can kill the body," Dan said, "but the One who can kill the soul. By trusting Christ, your soul is saved forever."

For more than an hour, they had shared scriptures with Nilikaanta. He had taken in every story they told him, quiet and solemn. His eyes were gleaming with tears. Now he pulled in a deep, shuddering breath and lifted his gaze to Dan and Tricia. "I will trust this Jesus," he said determinedly.

Dan and Tricia stood beside him, laying their hands on his shoulders, while Nilikaanta prayed to accept Jesus into his life—no matter what the cost. When Nilikaanta lifted his head, the worry and fear were gone from his eyes. Instead, joy radiated from him, the joy that only comes from knowing Jesus.

Dan was overwhelmed. All his life Nilikaanta had grown up worshiping the Hindu gods. Only yesterday had he heard about Jesus for the first time, and now, after a few hours of conversation, he was willing to give up everything—his way of life, his family, his livelihood, even his life—to follow Jesus.

Nothing but supernatural power could convince a person to believe in anything in this way.

God alone brings people to Himself, Dan thought, as he looked at Nilikaanta's smiling face. *It has nothing to do with the words of believers.* Dan felt a tremor of awe run through him. *Thank You, Lord, for allowing us the privilege of being Your ambassadors on earth.*

Storytelling for Life

The EvangeCube makes sharing the story of Jesus easy! Parents, Kids, Pastors, Youth Leaders, Sunday School Teachers, Missionaries, Lay Leaders and more can share this creative, easy-to-use puzzle to bring the Gospel of Jesus Christ to life.

Along with EvangeCube, e3 Resources provide a variety of tools that include a line of cause-based, education cubes aimed at fighting some of the world's toughest health and humanitarian issues. Helping people around the world to have a lasting and profound impact on countless lives.

e3resources.org

A Wild Ride

Dan skated around the rink, batting a ball back and forth with another man. They were in Dallas for a wedding, but before the day of the ceremony everyone was enjoying some fun playing broomball on the ice. After a rousing game, Dan and his new friend began to chat.

As the conversation went on, Dan found out that the man was a missionary. He was going to be leaving soon for Albania.

"Albania," Dan mused. "Where is that?"

"It's a small country near Greece," the man told him, working to untie his skates. "For years it's been under the rule of a fierce dictator. He made Albania completely atheistic and killed anyone of faith—Christians, Muslims, and all other followers of any belief system. No one was allowed in or out of Albania. It was shut off from the world."

"How are you going to get in, then?" Dan asked.

"Well, Albania has suddenly opened up. The dictator died a few years ago, and since then about 700 missionaries have been raised up to go and share the gospel with the Albanians." The man smiled. "The body of believers has been praying for Albania for a long time. It is truly an answer to prayer to be able to go there as a missionary."

"That's great," Dan said, inspired by the account of how God was moving. "I would love to become involved with your ministry."

"Of course!" the man said emphatically. "Anytime you want to come, I'd love to get in touch with you."

A short while later, Dan and a team of short-term missionaries were flying to Albania to partner with the national believers: dedicated people who were working hard to spread the name of Jesus in a country where God had been declared dead. Dan and the team flew into the main city of Tirana, where they met up with the local missionaries. Then the two teams banded together and set out for the remote cities that they had planned to visit.

To get there, the team was given an old van and a 19-year-old driver. Dan viewed the combination warily. Few people in Albania knew how to drive, and fewer knew how to drive well. The country had not been using cars for very long at all. The vehicles themselves were poor, and the roads were scarred with potholes. Dan wasn't keen on entrusting their lives to the fresh-faced youth standing before them.

"Thank you for your willingness to help," Dan said. "But...I think I'll drive."

The boy hopped in the back with the rest of the team, and Dan, taking a breath, turned towards the driver's seat. The van wasn't in great condition. It looked pretty battered and rusted, but at least it would drive. Dan pulled open the door, and staggered backwards as it came off in his hands. Really not in great condition, he thought, as with a grunt of exertion he lowered the door to the ground.

Their departure was delayed until the door could be reattached, and then everyone squeezed back into the van again. There were 14 people crowded into the vehicle and not enough seats for everyone. Several people elected to sit on the luggage in the back, and by way of some squishing and discomfort the entire team managed to fit inside. Dan carefully opened the front door and climbed into the driver's seat.

"Alright, here we go," he said, as the engine sputtered and groaned to life. With a tired sway, the old vehicle ambled out onto the road.

Dan tried to avoid the potholes, but there were so many that it was inevitable for the van to intermittently bang down into one with a violent lurch. The bounce sent the people in the back sliding over the luggage and scrambling for handholds, while the people in the seats were alternately crushed to each side as the van rocked back out of the pothole.

Besides the terrible roads, there were ox carts everywhere, slowly driving down the road or across the road. Most people still didn't use cars. Dan gingerly pressed the gas, keeping his foot ready to brake whenever another ox cart came rolling up. What with the inching pace, and the constant cart and pedestrian traffic, and the rough, pitted terrain, it took them about eight hours to travel a distance that would have taken two and a half on the roads Dan was used to. For eight hours the team rattled around in the van, until their knees and elbows were numb from being hit against the sides of the van more times than they could count, and they were so tired that they just let themselves slide around or be crushed flat against the window when the van veered around a turn. They were more than ready to lie down in their hotel beds.

Finally, Dan drove the van into Gjirokastër. It was a beautiful, ancient city, with old buildings and cobblestone streets, and above, on a hill overlooking the city, a gorgeous castle was silhouetted against the setting sun. Everyone sighed dreamily as they pressed their faces against the windows of the van. The peaceful, beautiful scene relaxed their nerves, and in just a few minutes they would be checked into their hotel and safe for the night. The missionary Dan had met in Dallas had been in Gjirokastër just the day before to confirm the reservations.

"You don't have reservations," the hotel clerk informed them when they walked up to the front desk.

The team looked at the clerk helplessly. "But..." Dan said, "They were confirmed."

The clerk shrugged, looking over his papers again. "I'm sorry, but we're completely full. Every room is taken. You'll have to try somewhere else."

Dan turned wearily towards his team. "Let's see if there is another place in town."

They walked outside the hotel, into the gathering twilight. In a small, pitiful huddle, they all asked God to provide a place for them to sleep that night. Being out in the city without somewhere to stay was frightening. Albania was rife with anarchy and crime after the sudden fall of the dictatorship. As the light dropped even lower, not a few of the team members were beginning to get nervous.

"Lord, please show us a place where we can stay," Dan prayed. "Amen."

With painful grimaces, the team climbed back into the van. It was depressing to find their seats again after they had thought they were finally done driving. Everyone sat quietly, gazing glumly out the windows, as Dan began to guide the van up the narrow streets. It was starting to drizzle, and the sad little drops running down the glass did nothing to lift their moods.

The first hotel they found was a shady, dirty place, with scary-looking security guards who smirked at them as they walked to the front desk. The hotel did have vacant rooms, but the women on the team begged not to stay there and no one was in opposition with their request. The van drove on. By now it was getting quite dark. Dan was having trouble focusing on driving, and navigating the tiny streets of Gjirokastër was nerve-wracking. There were only a few spare inches on either side between the van and the buildings.

So, thinking that he might be more used to driving in such situations, Dan handed the wheel over to the Albanian 19-year-old. But it turned out that he had even less an idea of what he was doing that Dan did. Dan gripped the side of the vehicle as the teenager powered the van up a steep cobblestoned hill. The roads were slick with rain, and Dan's heart leapt every time the wheels slid on the mossy stones.

With a vroom, the van gained the hill and then began to descend. The vehicle gathered speed, racing down the street, the buildings flashing past in a blur.

"Slow down!" Dan called, trying to tap the young driver on the shoulder.

"The brakes aren't working!" he shouted back. He struggled to maintain hold of the wheel as the van continued to speed up, the wheels spinning out of control on the rainy stones.

Dan swallowed hard. The rest of the team was starting to yell in fear, hanging onto their seats to keep from toppling out of them.

Suddenly one of the team shouted in panic, his face turning a sickly shade of white. "Look!"

The team followed his rigidly pointing finger and instantly gave a collective yell of terror. At the bottom of the hill, the street met the main road in a T-intersection. But just beyond that intersection was a cliff dropping several hundred feet off into night—straight ahead, directly in the path of the unstoppable vehicle.

Everyone was screaming, including the young driver, as the van barreled down the tiny street like a rocket down a chute. They zoomed out onto the main road and Dan threw up a prayer to heaven, along the lines of, "Lord Jesus, save us!" The cliff edge raced forwards. With a ferocious jerk, the teenager wrenched the wheel to the right, sending the vehicle skidding and sliding sideways across the road.

At the cliff's edge the van teetered for a moment in its forward impetus, tilting to the side. Then it gently settled back onto the road. The driver leaned back in his seat, his eyes bulging. All the passengers heaved gigantic sighs of relief. Instantly they praised God and thanked Him for sparing their lives.

"How about I drive?" Dan laughed nervously.

They continued their drive around the city, asking at various stops for a recommendation of where to stay. Finally, they were directed to a lovely, old-fashioned bed-and-breakfast which had a few vacant rooms. The pretty, quaint stone building was far nicer than even the first hotel had been, and the staff were pleasant and welcoming. Exhausted by the journey and the frights of the day, the team staggered to their rooms, thanking God for His protection and provision. They were asleep within moments.

In a Place Without God

Dan woke up the next morning to the sound of bleating goats.

Rising, he walked to the window of his room and looked out at the soft, misty morning. A hunched old man was driving a herd of goats down the cobblestone street outside. Their cloven hooves pattered across the stones, blending with their plaintive bleats as they headed out to pasture.

Dan took a deep breath, letting all the stress and worries of the day before fade away. The air was cool and fresh through the open window. Some distance away, Dan could see the city rising up in turrets of old stone. On the hill, the magnificent castle, wreathed in golden daylight, stood over everything like a silent sentinel. But beyond the city, the great, jagged mountains reared their heads—the true guardians of the land, capped with eternal snow.

The rest of the team seemed equally affected by the peaceful, pleasant atmosphere in which they had awakened. The bed-and-breakfast was a lovely spot. The building itself was beautiful, formed of old-fashioned stone buttresses and nestled contentedly in the midst of verdant, pastoral countryside.

Following breakfast, the team gathered for prayer and devotions. At least, they tried to. There was no meeting room at the bed-and-breakfast which could hold them all, so for that morning they had to make do with squishing into a hallway. Afterwards, they resolved to keep an eye out for another place where they could all meet together.

That day the team went into the city and visited the house of the Albanian dictator, Enver Hoxha, who had passed away several years earlier. His home had been turned into a museum. Dan and the team walked through the hallways and down one corridor where they came across a large, quiet room. A display sign named it the birthplace of the dictator himself.

The team paid the 25 cents per head admission and walked into the room. It was silent and spacious, with cushions spread along every wall. As they walked about in the room, more than a few of the team were trying to catch Dan's eye with a significant glance. He hid a smile, knowing what they were thinking. He was thinking it too.

"This looks like the perfect place to have our devotionals!" he said.

It only cost 25 cents a day to get in. Would the museum allow them to come and meet in the birth room?

Dan went up to the museum curator and asked, "Could we use that room every morning to meet in? We'll be here for a week."

After talking with a supervisor, the museum curator said "yes."

The team thanked God for His provision, and the next morning, they met at the museum and began their devotionals in the dictator's birth room. They used the room all week, holding small worship services and prayer times and training sessions there. As they lifted praise to Jesus, Dan was struck by the irony of the situation. *The dictator must be turning over in his grave,* he thought. Here they were, worshiping the one true Lord and Savior in the room where this man, who had declared God non-existent for over 40 years, had been born.

The missionaries' work in Albania was well received. People seemed starved for the truth, after living so long under a rule which forbade any worship of God, and many came to Christ. In one area, the team set up a meeting place and invited the townsfolk to hear the gospel. But when they had invited everyone, they realized there weren't enough chairs for everyone to sit on! So Dan walked next door to a local bar to hunt out some benches.

Inside were a bunch of men playing pool. Soon Dan had jumped into a game and was making friends with the locals, chatting good-naturedly and exchanging competitive shots. He invited them to the meeting next door. The men seemed interested, and as a group they decided to attend.

"We don't have any more chairs," Dan said. "Do you think the owner of the bar would let us borrow his?"

The men got permission and hauled bar-stools and benches out of the tavern and across to the meeting area. Then, at the gathering, they heard the gospel and accepted Jesus as their Savior. Afterwards the men helped the team carry all the bar-stools back to the tavern, but now as changed men.

Almost 600 people professed faith in Christ during the team's stay in Gjirokastër, and four new churches were started. It was incredible to see the gospel taking root in this strongly atheistic country, where people who had thought God was dead were now experiencing new life in Him through Christ Jesus. Soon, however, it came time for Dan's team and the nationals to go their separate ways.

Dan and the others were heading back to America, but they left one man behind. He was a Southern Baptist journeyman who had come with them on the trip. He would be staying in Albania for two years, helping to further the work that had been done in Gjirokastër and to disciple the new believers. There was a lot of hard work ahead for him. As the team said their goodbyes, the lone journeyman looked a little doleful.

"We'll be praying for you," Dan said, with his hand on the young man's shoulder.

The journeyman smiled. "Thanks. We'll all need it."

The team piled into their van and drove off towards the airport, leaving the journeyman to begin his new mission in Albania.

Over time, more journeymen began working in Albania to help establish new churches and encourage the young believers in their faith. A while after his team had returned to America, Dan received an email update from one of the journeymen who was stationed in a city that the team had visited.

The man wrote, "We've run out of space in our meeting place again, even as we were praising God for providing a bigger room! Now we are asking for His direction in finding a still larger place to hold our meetings."

The email continued to tell of a Muslim family the journeyman had been witnessing to: "I also had an encounter with the father of two girls who had accepted Christ. He is a Muslim, so I was unsure what to expect when I came to talk to him. He told me, 'All my daughters want to do now is talk about Jesus and read the Bible!' His girls smiled when he said that. I spent some time talking with the father and explained to him what had changed his daughters' hearts. He listened, and when I finished he said, 'Thank you for coming and telling me what you are teaching my daughters. They may attend your meetings.' I had thought that there might be some trouble with this Muslim father. But he has actually offered to help us find a new place in which to meet."

The journeyman's note concluded with, "Again, I thank you for your prayers and continued support. God is working in Albania. Blessings to you all."

Into the Lion's Den

Manipur, India. A place torn by riots and terrorist attacks, filled with chaos and danger, as it had been when e3 Partners had first visited. Now the situation there had become so bad that martial law was declared in hope of somehow quelling the havoc. But in Manipur there were still many tribes who hadn't heard the gospel. So naturally, Manipur was the place where Dan Hitzhusen and the rest of his team were flying to at that very moment.

The team had spent much time in prayer and had received advice from knowledgeable Christian leaders before deciding to go on the trip. In the end, they believed God was calling them to this state despite the unrest. And, as they had been told, an area under martial law was actually safer because of the many officers and soldiers armed and on patrol.

After 26 hours of traveling, the team of missionaries landed in Calcutta, the capital of India. They spent a quick night in a hotel, and the next morning they drove back to the airport to catch their flight to Manipur. But before they left the hotel, Dan led a devotional. He talked about 1 Peter 5:8: "Be of sober spirit, be on the alert. Your adversary, the devil, prowls around like a roaring lion, seeking someone to devour."

Satan was a lion, waging a battle against them, and Dan reminded his team that they would face spiritual warfare, especially on this important trip.

At the airport, Dan picked up a copy of *The Indian Times.* The title of one of the articles flashed up at him in bold letters: Manipur—In the Lion's Den. Dan looked at the pictures of rioters, and dead bodies, and soldiers carrying machine guns, and felt morbidly amused by the obvious connection. They already knew that Satan was a roaring lion; now it appeared that they were entering the lion's den itself.

When they finally arrived in Manipur, Peter and Moala Kashung eagerly greeted them with the statement, "Our Daniels are here!" It was both a reference to Daniel's bravery and to the fact that there were two men named Dan on this trip, but the team identified more with the feeling of being tossed into the hungry mouths of Daniel's beasts, referencing the story from the Old Testament. Had it really been wise to come here?

Because of the martial law that had been instated, each team member was assigned a Central Intelligence Department (CID) agent to act as their bodyguard. Dan's agent was a serious-faced fellow, armed with a motley assortment of guns. He would follow the team wherever they went and protect them from everything he could.

It was now too dangerous to travel to the Meitei tribe, so Peter had decided that the team would begin ministering to the Rongmei tribe. They were another lost people group who worshipped many different gods—ancestral gods, local village gods, and personal family gods. Dan and the others, on their first day, went into a small village and simply began sharing the gospel. The CID agent stayed close by, his gun at the ready, expecting things to go wrong quickly.

But at the village, the missionaries were met with nothing but favor. The Rongmei welcomed them and listened enthusiastically as the gospel was shared. Dan prayed over many of them, and there were some miraculous healings. People prayed to accept Christ and worshipped Him with tears in their eyes.

At the next village it was the same way. Another team member shared the gospel. The CID agent stood nearby. He heard the truth spoken and saw the power it had to change these people's hearts. He saw the power of God to heal sickness and injury. He saw the boldness with which these missionaries entered each village—villages where they should be frightened, villages where, realistically, there could be attacks at any moment. But they were not afraid.

As Dan walked through one of the villages, a drunken man staggered towards them, holding several stones in his hands. Dan felt the CID agent tense beside him. Dan just calmly kept on walking. The man could barely keep on his feet; when he threw one of the rocks at Dan, it fell short and thudded into the dust. The agent watched as Dan disregarded the attack, his face relaxed and friendly. Then the agent quietly walked over and took the rocks out of the man's hands, calmed him down and sent him away.

The first day passed. Dan's team had gone into several different Rongmei villages and had seen God moving in amazing ways. Everyone had remained safe. Apart from the one man who was too drunk to even think clearly, all the villagers had shown nothing but acceptance and eagerness. Their favor towards these foreigners was not normal. There was something more, something supernatural, that accompanied the missionaries and provided them with perfect protection.

Dan and the others gathered together in the morning, laughing and sharing stories from the day before, and talking about which villages they would visit next. As they chatted, Dan saw the CID agent come slowly into the room. There was no sign of the guns he usually had with him all the time. Instead, there was a young girl at his side.

The agent met Dan's gaze from across the room.

Dan stood up and walked over to his bodyguard. The CID agent whispered to the girl, squeezing her hand briefly. When Dan stopped in front of him, the agent raised his eyes.

"I have guarded the Pope," the agent said steadily. "And the Prime Minister of India."

Dan nodded, unsure of how this conversation had come about or where it was heading.

The agent swallowed. "When I went out with you yesterday…I was armed to the teeth. I thought there would be trouble. But now…" He spread his hands wide, his serious eyes deep and blazing. "I realize. The God you serve is more powerful than any weapon I can carry."

He reached for the girl's hand again and said to Dan, "This is my daughter. I want her to come with us, so she, too, can hear the Word you bring."

Dan searched for words to say. "Yes," he finally managed. "She must come."

As the team went from village-to-village, just as they had done before, the agent and his daughter sat together, listening to the gospel being preached. They talked together in their soft, serious voices. Halfway through the day, when Dan offered an invitation for the villagers to pray to Jesus, both the CID agent and his daughter raised their hands, along with many other villagers. Dan couldn't hold back his smile.

What could weapons of men do compared to the presence of God surrounding them? There, in the middle of the lion's den, they were absolutely safe.

Did you know that UnveilinGLORY
creates Homeschool Curricula for students
from Kindergarten through 12th grade?

www.UnveilinGLORY.com/Homeschool

A Time to Dance

In Manipur, one of the villages Dan's team worked in was a Rongmei village called Majorkuhl. As the team would joke, "It was a major cool place." The Indian CID agent accompanied them, as he did to every location, to provide them with protection—but now he was also eager see what God was doing and to learn more about Him.

In Majorkuhl, Dan met a woman named Mrs. Paomei. Mrs. Paomei was a Christian. She had married an unbeliever, who had promised to become a Christian once they were wed. But, twenty years later, her husband still refused to acknowledge Christ. Mrs. Paomei had faithfully raised all her children in the truth, and they had all accepted Christ as their Savior. All of them, Mrs. Paomei and her seven children, prayed constantly for Mr. Paomei's heart to be changed, so that he, like them, could have the joy of knowing Jesus.

The Paomei family had suffered much. Not only was Mr. Paomei not a Christian, Mrs. Paomei and her children were the only Christians in their village. Everyone else in Majorkuhl worshipped ancestral gods, as well as village gods and family gods. So whenever something bad happened, they would blame Mrs. Paomei.

"It's your fault," they would say. "You have upset the gods, and now they are punishing us."

Mrs. Paomei was beaten, spit upon, fined numerous times, and shunned by her community. But still, through all this, she remained faithful to her Lord and strong in her faith.

When Dan's team came to Majorkuhl, the first thing they did was go to Mrs. Paomei's house to share the gospel with her husband. For twenty years, Mrs. Paomei had been a living witness to him, and he had not listened to her. But Dan and Peter Kashung, the key Indian leader and Dan's interpreter, hoped that God could use them to open his heart to Jesus.

For Mr. Paomei, having an American visit his house was a great honor. In that area Americans were considered super-caste, at the very top of the social ranks. He graciously invited Dan, Peter, and their team into his house.

Peter explained why they were there, and then he and Dan began to share the gospel with Mr. Paomei. For two and a half hours they spoke with him. They pleaded with him to see the truth, to see the relationship his family had with Jesus that filled their lives with such joy and peace. Mr. Paomei seemed hesitant, as if he wanted to believe, but had held back too long.

At last Dan fell silent, unsure of what else to say.

"Let me talk to him," Peter said quietly.

Dan nodded. Peter turned to Mr. Paomei and began conversing in the local language. Dan couldn't understand a word of what was going on, but from the expressions on the two men's faces and the tone in their voices, he could tell that it was an intense discussion.

For twenty minutes Peter talked with Mr. Paomei. As Peter spoke, Mr. Paomei's face became weary, losing its guarded expression and becoming more and more open. His tone lowered, and his words were soft. At last, in response to a query from Peter, Mr. Paomei nodded.

Peter smiled at Dan. "He is ready to pray."

Mr. Paomei got down on his knees, and Dan knelt with him and clasped Mr. Paomei's hands. Behind them, Mrs. Paomei and all her children gathered around. Sobbing desperately, they watched as Mr. Paomei bowed his head. After twenty years, twenty years of praying and mourning for him, the family was watching their prayers being answered. Was it any wonder that they wept with joy?

Dan led Mr. Paomei in prayer. In the humblest of prayers, with his eyes filled with tears, the man who had refused Christ for so long asked Him to be His Lord and Savior. And when Mr. Paomei opened his eyes, his weary look had vanished. Instead, there burned within him a joy that transformed his entire countenance.

Mr. Paomei couldn't even get up from the floor before his family had thrown themselves at him, nearly knocking him down. The children hugged him tightly, Mrs. Paomei had her arms around his neck, and the entire family was laughing and crying and shouting with joy.

Dan and Peter watched the happy scene with a warm glow in their hearts. The family was finally united in Christ.

But God's work was not yet done in the Paomei's house. Shortly after Mr. Paomei accepted Christ, two girls, the children's cousins, came over. The family excitedly pulled them inside, too full of happiness to hold in what had happened. Then the cousins wanted to know what the visitors had told Mr. Paomei. Dan and Peter shared the gospel again, and the two girls asked Jesus to be their Savior as well.

When the two girls returned home, their father heard what had happened. He went over to the Paomei's house in a towering rage.

"What have you told my girls?" he asked, glaring at Dan and Peter. "What's going on here?"

Dan cast a glance at Peter. "Let us tell you what we told them," he said.

Soon afterwards, the father was heading home to his girls—as a new believer in Jesus.

The word spread around the village, and more people came to the Paomei's house to hear the gospel. One man came who had terrible scars and wounds covering his back.

"I was accused of selling my friend into slavery," he said bitterly, showing Dan and Peter the brutal marks on his body. "I didn't. But the village beat me with canes until I fell unconscious."

Dan dropped his eyes in sympathy, knowing the pain and anger the man must be feeling. "You know," he said slowly, "Jesus was beaten for things he didn't do."

Tears shone in the man's eyes as he looked up at Dan.

"You can worship a God who knows where you've been," Dan said, giving the man a small smile.

The man nodded. A smile started to spread across his own face. "I'd like to do that," he whispered.

By the end of the team's time in Majorkuhl, a church was able to be started in the Paomei's home. At the closing service, before Dan and Peter and the rest of the missionaries had to leave, all the new believers came together and celebrated. Mr. Paomei even stood up before the crowd and shared his testimony.

"I know now," he said, beaming, "what it means to know Jesus. I know the joy of having Him as my Lord!"

The church shouted praise to God, and in the midst of the worship, Mrs. Paomei got up and started dancing.

Dan watched her worship with perfect happiness on her face. *For 20 years she's been waiting,* he thought. *She's endured such persecution from her village, and she's been praying without answer for so many years, without any other believers around her to support her. Now look at what God has done.*

    Now, Mrs. Paomei's husband was proclaiming the Name of the Lord, her relatives were worshiping Jesus, and a church had been started in her home. As Dan thought about it, he couldn't hold his joy in any longer. He leapt to his feet, and though he'd never been much of a dancer, he began to dance alongside Mrs. Paomei. For the Bible says there is a time to mourn and a time to dance. And if ever there was a time to dance, this was it—to celebrate the answer to a faithful family's prayer, the salvation of these new believers, the birth of a church, and the great and glorious Name of the Lord who gives abundant life.

Families on Mission

Family mission trips offer a unique opportunity for parents to invest in their kids' spiritual lives by serving together. Just by setting aside one week, your family can explore a new culture, introduce the Gospel to new people, and establish new churches.

With e3 Legacy, you and your family serve together by helping local churches strengthen their communities and promote the Gospel. Your kids even run daily Bible clubs that share Christ with other children in the community. Families that serve together make a profound impact on the lives of those around them.

e3 Legacy partners with many great ministries and is an official partner of Dr. James Dobson's Family Talk.

e3partners.org/causes/legacy

My Best Friend Jesus

Dan had returned to Manipur again with another team of volunteer missionaries. In every village the team visited, people came flooding out to meet them. The Americans among the team were a strange sight to them with their light-colored skin and accents—so different from any people the villagers had seen before. Huge crowds gathered around the team. Everyone wanted to get a glimpse of the foreigners and greet them.

Many people in Manipur had never heard the Name of Jesus. They didn't even have a passing knowledge of the Bible or of God's love. That's why the team had come. The believers were here to tell them about the one true God and His great love for mankind.

The villagers heard the gospel with awe. It was a beautiful, beautiful truth to their ears—a message new and radical, but one that resonated so deeply with their souls. They received the Good News with rejoicing and worship. Even though persecution was a constant threat in Manipur, and a new Christian would be a target for attacks and troubles, many people with whom the team shared the gospel, professed faith in Jesus Christ. There was nothing holding them back. Why would they refuse the precious gift of forgiveness and life? Why would they reject a loving, merciful, and just God who wanted to save them?

All they needed was to hear from someone, anyone, who was bearing God's Word.

As the team ministered among the villagers, Dan spoke with two young men from the Meitei tribe.

"Jesus is the Way, the Truth, and the Life," Dan said. "He is the only way to the Father—to the one true God."

"We want to know Him," one of the young men said firmly. The other nodded his agreement.

Kneeling beside them, Dan recognized again the huge privilege God had granted to him and all the missionaries to share the gospel with the lost. He led the two men in prayer as they both accepted Christ as their Savior.

When they raised their heads, one of the men grasped Dan's hand. "Please. Can you tell us about Jesus?"

At first Dan was confused. What did they want to know? He was sure they had understood the salvation message.

The man persisted. "Please tell us more. You know him. What is he like?"

Then Dan realized. These men didn't want to know about salvation. They wanted to know more about Jesus—like a friend they had just met and now wanted to get to know better.

Dan stood up. "Come. Let me tell you about my best friend, Jesus."

The sky was a dusky blue overhead. The sunlight shimmered in the air, its heat tingling Dan's skin. As was the custom of that area, the two young men held Dan's hands as they walked out onto the dusty road. Dan, an American, felt a little uncomfortable holding the two men's hands. But they were so sincere as they waited for him to speak that Dan continued to hold on.

"Jesus performed many miracles on earth," Dan began. "He sought out the weak, the young, the sick, and the sinners. He was loving and compassionate."

The Meitei men smiled. This was the God they had surrendered their lives to.

"God wants you to learn about Him through His word, and talk to Him through prayer," Dan went on. "He wants to have a relationship with you." Dan looked from one man to the other. "God promises that He will never leave you."

As they walked, a few villagers passed them on the road, their ever-curious eyes studying Dan's strange appearance. And all around was the flat, dusty ground which no foreigner had set foot on for many years.

The moment swelled Dan's heart. God had brought him to Manipur and given him the opportunity to speak the Name of Jesus to these men for the very first time. Now, in the peaceful afternoon with the sun gently descending from the sky, Dan walked down the long, winding path in the heart of Manipur, clasping hands with his new Indian brothers and telling them about his best friend, Jesus.

The 28 Day Journey

Dan and a team from e3 Partners were in India, holding a church planting training seminar for the nationals. From the neighboring country of Burma—now called Myanmar—a small group of local Christians made an eight-day journey, on foot, to attend the training. In that two-day period of discipleship they grew and learned so much that they begged Dan to come to their homeland.

"Come and teach us in Burma," they pleaded. "Come partner in our ministry."

Burma was a military dictatorship and a stronghold of Buddhism. There was much strife and persecution for Christians. In fact, e3 Partners had never gone to Burma before. It was a rather scary place for them.

But Dan promised the Burmese: "I'll pray and by God's grace we will come and help you."

They smiled in relief and excitement. "Thank you. Thank you!"

Dan went back to America and discussed a trip to Burma with the e3 staff. They listened to the story of the Burmese Christians and agreed that e3 Partners should go over and help them. But before e3 Partners would send teams to any new country, they would always send a member of their staff to that country to provide training to the national believers. After these local believers had been trained and had developed their vision for ministry, then an e3 team would come and partner with them to help get their vision started.

Mike, an e3 Partners leader, was set to leave for Burma to hold the training. But suddenly—he couldn't go. And there was no email or phone service in Burma. Mike tried to reach the Burmese Christians to tell them that the training couldn't happen, but he couldn't get through. So, unknowingly, the Burmese began the long journey to reach the training.

It was a seven-day journey to reach the site of the training: four days walking and three days riding on the tops of buses. The journey on foot was unpleasant and even treacherous. The believers had to sleep on the side of the road at night and cover themselves with palm leaves to keep the mosquitoes off. Bandits prowled the roads, putting them at risk of robbery and injury. Tigers, too, were common in the areas where they had to travel. After that, there were still three more days crammed onto public transportation—all for two days of training. But when the Burmese believers arrived, sweaty and exhausted, there was no one to teach them. The only thing they could do was to turn around and make the seven-day journey back to their homes.

Mike and Dan felt terrible. These people had undertaken a long, hard journey to get this training, and there had been no one to give it to them. Dan had to try again—the Burmese Christians wanted this teaching so badly! He resolved to do everything he possibly could to make sure they got it. Somehow, Dan and a team would go to Burma and hold another training seminar.

However, for a month there was no communication with the nationals. Dan had made the preparations for the trip, but he couldn't contact the local Burmese and find out if they knew the team was coming. And the visa he had ordered hadn't come in like it was supposed to.

The day of their flight to Burma arrived. That morning, Dan had to pick up his visa from the FedEx office where it had just arrived and then make it to the Los Angeles airport in under two hours. Just leaving the United States seemed like an impossible task. What would happen when they got to Burma?

When Dan had collected the visa, he tore off towards the airport. With much prayer and a few miles-per-hour over the speed limit, he made it to the airport on time. He had no complications getting through security, he found the gate where the team was waiting, and their plane left on time. Now the team could sit back and start to pray again. They didn't know if any of their messages had gotten through to the nationals. Would there be someone waiting for them at the airport? Or would the team find themselves alone in the foreign country, without knowing anyone, in a place where Christians were not welcomed?

The plane landed on schedule. Dan and the team grabbed their luggage, exchanging bolstering looks, and shuffled off the airplane.

Dan emerged from the gate into a mass of people. On every side, eager faces peered over signs that welcomed various passengers to the country. Dan looked from side to side, searching for any sign of someone who might be at the airport for them. He wouldn't recognize the local Christians by appearance, even if they were there; Dan had never met them before.

The bobbing white signs almost made Dan dizzy. There were strangers everywhere, and strange names. There was no one to meet them—but then! Squeezing under a man's elbow and waving frantically, a Burmese man popped up near the rail—brandishing a sign that read "Dan Hitzhusen."

Dan blew out a big sigh of relief. "It's good to see you," Dan said emphatically as he shook hands with the Burmese believer.

The man smiled broadly. "Thank you for coming. The people have already started the journey to attend the training."

Dan was amazed yet again by the determination of these people. Not to be deterred by one disappointment, they were willingly and enthusiastically making the same arduous, seven-day journey again.

The team set up the training seminar, and a few days afterwards the people began arriving. Despite the dirt and sweat and fear and toil of their travels, there was nothing but smiles on their faces. For two days, they had the chance to be instructed and discipled and to grow their ministry. What was their journey compared to that?

At the end of the training, Dan watched the Burmese believers begin straggling off down the road, each group heading back to their own homes. By the time they completed the return journey, they would have traveled a total of 28 days—16 of those days on foot—seeking the two days of Biblical training. Dan could hardly believe it. The commitment and desire of these national believers was astounding. He couldn't wait to begin ministry with them.

Unexplainable

The windows of the van had been covered with towels so no one could look inside. With a gentle lurch the vehicle came to a stop, and one of the national believers pulled open the door.

"Come inside, quickly," he said in a low voice.

Dan ducked his head down as he climbed out of the van, moving swiftly and silently over the short distance between the vehicle and the building. His teammate, Debbie, was close behind him. The national Christian leader watched up and down the street as Dan and Debbie hurried past. When they were inside, he calmly walked after them and shut the door.

"We are neighbors with the local authorities," the national said as he closed up a low window. "They will tolerate foreigners being here—as long as no one of higher rank finds out. Then we'll be on our own to face the consequences. Better to keep out of sight." Dan and Debbie, as Americans, would only risk being thrown out of the country if they were caught. The nationals would be thrown in jail, or even killed. But for the sake of reaching their people with the gospel, they were willing to suffer.

Inside the large room of the building, Dan's eyes adjusted to the dim light. Thirty Burmese Buddhists were sitting on the floor, waiting. The national Christian leader came up behind him.

"We invited them all personally," he said softly. "They are ready to hear the gospel." Dan nodded and stepped forward, with Debbie at his side.

It was their first day of ministry after the training in Burma. The national believers had arranged discreet locations where the teams could speak, and they had brought together select groups of people to listen. Then the nationals drove teams of two or three of the Americans to each building. There was an atmosphere of tension and secrecy over the proceedings, weighing down like an ever-present burden.

"Hello! My name is Dan," Dan greeted the Burmese.

"And my name is Debbie," his teammate said, smiling pleasantly. The gathered crowd smiled in return, exchanging greetings with the visitors.

"We've come to tell you about Jesus," Dan said.

Dan and Debbie shared their testimonies, and from there they had an open path to share the gospel. They explained that God was the one true God and that He had sent His Son, Jesus, as a sacrifice for the sins of man. Then Dan extended an invitation to the Buddhists to accept this sacrifice Jesus had made on their behalf. "Would you like to ask Jesus to be your Lord and Savior?" he asked.

Every hand in the room went up.

A surge of joy swept through Dan, and, with a huge smile, he said, "Then let's pray."

The morning passed rapidly. Lunch was served, and Dan and Debbie enjoyed a time of laughter and happiness as they talked with the 30 Burmese who had professed faith in Christ. After the meal, the people asked Dan and Debbie to pray for them. Of course, they agreed.

The first man hobbled forward on a crutch. His entire right side was paralyzed and both his right arm and leg were shrunken and limp. He dragged half of his body behind him as he walked up to Dan and Debbie.

Debbie laid her hands on the man, and began to pray. Dan grasped the man's hand. It was withered and unresponsive; the man had been paralyzed for so long that there was no life in the limb whatsoever.

"Please, reveal Your glory, Lord," Debbie prayed. "Show Your mighty power in this man's body and heal him. Dan clasped the man's hand tightly, whispering in agreement with Debbie's plea.

A finger twitched against his own.

Dan stiffened and glanced at the hand he was holding. Slowly, fractionally, the fingers were starting to curl upwards. Dan felt energy returning to the limb, flowing through the muscles that had lain dead and waking the nerves. Then the hand gripped Dan's wrist.

"Debbie," Dan breathed. The man stared at his own hand, as if unable to believe that the limb belonged to his body.

Debbie opened her eyes and took in a sharp breath. The man's eyes were brimming with tears. He pressed Dan's hand tighter, and a faint laugh escaped his lips. He stepped back and planted his weight solidly on his right leg. It was no longer limp and withered, but whole.

"Praise Jesus!" the man sobbed. He raised his right arm into the air, as far as he could reach. "I'm healed!"

Dan and Debbie stood together, watching the man rejoice. "Whoa," Dan said softly. Debbie nodded. Her hands were trembling.

"Please, will you pray for my wife?" the man begged, grasping Dan's hand again.

"Yes, of course," Dan said hurriedly. The man veritably bounded away, and returned leading his wife. As the woman lifted her head, Dan saw that her eyes were completely white. She was blind.

The man tenderly set his wife's hands on Debbie's arm. "These people are going to pray for you," he whispered to her.

Rather shakily, Debbie laid her hands on the woman's eyes, and Dan put his on the woman's shoulders. They were both still recovering from the display of power in the man's healing. Would God choose to heal again? They didn't know.

"Display Your glory," Dan prayed. "Please heal this woman in Your Name and by Your almighty power."

"Amen," Debbie said. She lifted her hands from the woman's face.

Two brilliant blue eyes gazed back at her, as pure as the summer sky.

The woman stared at Dan and Debbie and then at her husband, her mouth parted in shock. "I can...see," she said, in the barest whisper. "I can see again!"

Debbie felt herself swaying, and quickly caught her balance. *The blind had been healed.*

The woman threw her arms around her husband, crying and shouting praise to Jesus. Dan stepped back, his heart pounding. He had just witnessed a clear, demonstrative miracle, and his mind could barely process it.

Now more people came forward seeking prayer. One was a woman who had been troubled for months with a stomach virus, which none of the doctors could cure. Someone had suggested that she come to the Christian gathering—maybe they would be able to help her. Dan gathered some of the new believers around the woman and had them lay their hands on her as well, joining Dan and Debbie in prayer.

But as they prayed, the woman began to writhe and twist with an unnatural strength. She opened her mouth and screamed—in a man's voice. Dan felt a chill run up his back, and he knew they were dealing with more than a stomach illness. The woman was demon-possessed.

"Lord, glorify Your Name!" Dan prayed. He held onto the woman's shoulders as she continued to struggle, her face contorted into strange, terrible expressions. "Remove the sickness from this woman and drive out the spirits in her in the Name of Jesus and by His shed blood on the cross. They have no place here!"

The woman froze and let out a horrible scream of terror and wickedness. "They're coming for us!" she shouted. As if a cord had been cut, she collapsed in the believers' arms, unconscious.

Dan helped lay the woman down, and the new believers placed a pillow under her head.

"This is getting weirder by the minute," Debbie said with a breathless laugh. Her face was pale. Dan nodded, sure that his own countenance was no better than hers.

They prayed for many more people, and, except for one young man, God healed all of them. Dan and Debbie didn't know why God had chosen not to heal the one man. He had been devoutly fasting and praying for the ministry, and in the process his body had shut down so that he had lost almost all capabilities. But this faithful believer God did not heal. It was a reminder that each miracle God performs has a purpose—as do those that He does not.

Dan and Debbie spent the entire day, from morning until night, at that home, discipling the new believers. After about an hour the unconscious woman had awakened. She stayed with the group until they began to disperse, and then she quietly went home to her own house.

That night, for the very first time, she made dinner for her husband.

As Dan and Debbie climbed into the van, leaving the excited, chattering crowd behind, their sense of reason began kicking in.

"That couldn't have just happened," Dan said. "Did that really just happen?"

It was too much to process. They had seen so much supernatural power displayed and so many miracles worked, that it seemed more logical to their strained minds that they had dreamed the entire experience. Even though they had witnessed it with their own eyes, they were having trouble believing it.

The other teams had seen huge numbers of healings as well. One American woman had prayed for a little girl who had a tumor the size of a golfball growing from her chest. The woman didn't even know what to pray. It seemed inevitable that the child would die. But she bowed her head and asked God to do what would be best for the little girl. The next day, the tumor was gone and the child was running about again, laughing with a carefree and innocent joy.

Incidentally, these teams were all from a church that generally believed that God didn't perform miracles anymore! But as they prayed in Jesus' name, they saw amazing, unexplainable wonders occur. God was still at work through the faith of His servants—no matter how small that faith was.

The Greatest Miracle

By the next day, word had gotten out about the healings and miracles that had taken place at the Christian gathering. When Dan and Debbie returned to the house in the morning, the number of Buddhists within the room had greatly increased.

Dan had never been surrounded by so many sick people. There were lepers, whose hands had been eaten away by the disease until their arms were mere stumps. There were people suffering from AIDs and heart disease and many other terrible illnesses. The woman who had been demon-possessed returned, this time bringing her husband with her, who was an alcoholic. He wanted to be set free from his addiction.

The faces of the people were strained with pain, grief, and suffering. As Dan stood up in front of them, he was moved by their awful plight. They had horrible sicknesses, and they had no hope.

"I'm going to tell you about my Lord," Dan said.

He shared his testimony, as he had the day before, and explained the gospel again. When he told them about Jesus' sacrifice and the free gift of salvation, all of the people professed faith in Christ. Then, as before, Dan and Debbie and the other believers began to pray for the sick and disabled.

They prayed just as fervently, with the same surrender to God to do as He willed, for His glory. But today, God chose not to heal. There were no demonstrative miracles. No limbs were suddenly restored to health. No sicknesses instantly vanished.

Finally, Dan turned to face the people. "I don't know why God chose not to heal today," he said slowly. "But what I do know is that when we worship—the things of earth growing strangely dim, in the light of His wonder and grace."

The whole crowd moved together, and the national Christians began to lead them in a time of worship. They had brought hymnals written in Burmese. These were passed throughout the crowd, and Dan listened as the song began to swell from the masses of people within the room. He recognized the melody, but there was something drastically different hearing it sung in the language of this country, from the lips of the people who had undergone such hardship—and who, for most, this was the first offering of worship they had ever given to the Lord.

They sang with everything in them. All their pain, all their gratitude, all their service, all their worship poured into the song, filling the room until it seemed to drive out the air. Dan and Debbie were overwhelmed by God's grace. They saw the woman who had been blind, now reading the words of the hymnal. They saw the man who had been paralyzed, raising his hands high in worship. And they saw, on every countenance, a sublime expression of peace. Most of the people were still suffering, they were still in pain, and they were still haggard and sick. But there was a glimmer of something in their eyes that had been missing before—hope. Their bodies were afflicted, but their souls had been healed. And somehow, they didn't seem to care so much about their illnesses anymore.

This crowd of young believers became a new church in that village. The national missionaries would disciple them and lead them, and in time, help them plant another church as an outpouring of their growth and ministry.

The other villages where Dan's team was working experienced amazing responses and miraculous occurrences as well. At one gathering, as a team member was sharing the gospel with a crowd, a king cobra slithered into their midst. These huge snakes were deadly and vicious. Whenever one appeared, it would strike people aggressively and kill them with its venom.

The team member had fallen silent, and the villagers froze. The cobra's tongue flickered from its pointed snout. Then, with a fluid, mesmerizing movement, the cobra began to wind between the people who were sitting to listen. They sat motionless, every muscle rigid with terror, as the snake undulated past them. For a few hideous moments no one said a word; the villagers were waiting for the snake to strike. The creature moved like a ripple of water flowing across the ground. It traveled through the entire crowd and then moved past, leaving the people behind.

The villagers looked up to the speaker, completely shaken and shocked. The king cobra never left without making a kill. It was a miracle. One by one the villagers began to raise their hands, acknowledging that Jesus was the One True God, and accepting Him as their Lord and the Savior of their souls.

At the end of the week, Dan's team held a celebration service, bringing together all the people from all the different villages who had experienced God's power and salvation. Dan asked several of the new believers, including many who had been supernaturally healed, to share their testimonies.

The wife and husband who had been healed stood up first. Dan expected to hear the story of their healing and the amazing wonders God had demonstrated. After all, wouldn't that be an incredible story to share?

But the man, his voice trembling with emotion, proclaimed an even more powerful cure. "The greatest miracle I have seen is how Jesus saved me," he said. "He granted me healing of my body, but it is my soul that rejoices, for Jesus has cleansed me from sin!"

Every person who had experienced a demonstrative miracle passed over their physical restoration, in order to praise God for their spiritual salvation. And those who had not been healed of sickness rejoiced with the same wonder, awe, and tearful gratitude as all the rest. Because of the demonstration of His healing power on the first day, God had drawn many more people to hear the gospel. Then all of them had been able to receive the greatest gift of all.

As for the nationals with whom Dan's team had been partnering, they were stunned speechless by the enormity of what God had done in just one week. They had hoped that maybe six Buddhists would come to know Christ. Instead, 332 former Buddhists had professed faith in Christ, 21 existing churches had been strengthened, and 5 new churches had been planted. The woman who had been demon-possessed and her alcoholic husband both began attending Bible school in preparation for joining the ministry.

The woman's husband did not seem to be healed at the time that Dan and his team prayed over him. But before a year had gone by, he was freed from his addiction and he and his wife were faithfully pursuing the Lord. God was continuing to work miracles—in personal, ordinary ways—long after that radical, unexplainable day in the building in Burma.

The Hotel Church

There was gold everywhere. Statues made of gold sat on the street corners; temples coated with gold stood in the city square; idols formed of gold were enthroned in households; altars inlaid with gold called families to prayer. Burma was a poverty-stricken land where many people were hungry and cold due to lack of money to buy themselves provisions. And yet there was gold everywhere.

Dan and a team of about 15 people had flown into Burma to partner with the local believers. The Burmese national missionaries had a vision to plant 40 house churches. It might have seemed like an unreasonable goal in this area where there were three million Buddhists and less than one percent were Christian. But, seeing the faith of the nationals and their complete trust in God for the task, the American team was greatly encouraged.

At their hotel, the staff welcomed them in English, wearing pleasant smiles. Dan and the team found their rooms, settled in, and then went for a leisurely walk around the city. Even in that short time, they could see the prominence of Buddhism. A well-known landmark, a gigantic statue of Buddha on his side, lay along the length of a city block. Outside one building, a small gathering of people were pouring water over the Holy Rat. And everywhere the team turned there was a temple. The buildings were extravagant, gold and jewel-encrusted shrines with vaulted ceilings and pillared entranceways, in stark contrast with the poor homes surrounding it. Dan viewed their expressions of worship sadly. How many more people would be able to afford food to eat if they stopped using their wealth to make idols and temples? How many would be able to live in peace and joy if they knew the truth?

Early the next morning, after prayer and devotions, the team members were picked up in motorized rickshaws and taken out into the city. They hoped, by the end of the week, to reach 40 homes with the gospel. Praying for God to speak through them, Dan led his small team up to the first home and knocked.

A young boy answered the door, his mother close behind him. The woman wore a strange type of make-up, which helped keep the disease-bearing mosquitoes away.

The national translator greeted them. "We would like to tell you about our God," he said in Burmese. The woman hesitated for a moment, and then invited the team into her house. The boy, his mother, and his older sister sat down on the floor as the team began sharing testimonies of how God had changed their lives.

"We are changed—because Jesus has saved us," one said. The family was curious. What did this mean? They listened intently as Dan shared the gospel. When he finished the story, the family was in tears. They asked to be led in prayer, and, with the team around them, all three knelt on the floor of their house to accept Christ.

"We will come back tomorrow," Dan told the family. "We'll teach you more about God, and show you how you can teach others." The mother, brother, and sister smiled at him, thanking the entire team for coming to tell them about Jesus.

The team went to many more houses, and at each home the response was powerful. Men, women, children, grandparents and families alike professed faith in Christ. After a few gospel presentations, Dan told the nationals to begin sharing their faith. Speaking in animated Burmese, the local missionaries preached Jesus' name to their countrymen and rejoiced with them when they accepted Christ into their lives.

By the end of the first day, they had reached over a dozen homes. They came back to the hotel, talking excitedly about what had occurred. The hotel staff watched them strangely. The staff understood English, and they could tell something exciting was going on.

The next day the team went out again and saw the same eager response to the gospel. People were desperate for the truth. The team also returned to the houses they had visited before, and led an *I Am Second* group, which taught the new believers to study the Bible and lead groups of their own. It was late at night when they finally got back to their hotel rooms. The clerk at the desk watched them enter the lobby, wondering what kept them out all day and brought them back both exhausted and exhilarated.

The week went by in a blur. Forty households responded to the gospel, and the team led first-time Bible studies in each one. They trusted that as the nationals discipled these gatherings of new believers, 40 new house churches would be started. The team also had the privilege of baptizing many of the people they had witnessed to. Several of their own team, who had never been baptized before, asked to proclaim their faith along with the young believers. It was a glorious, joyful experience.

By now the hotel staff had heard about the large numbers of people coming to Christ. They heard about the new churches and the baptisms and the resolve of the nationals to spread the gospel further. Late one night, when Dan and his team returned to the hotel, the staff finally stepped out and confronted them.

"Why have you been telling all these people about Jesus," the clerk said, her hands on her hips, "And you haven't told us?"

"We want to know what is changing everyone's hearts," a bellhop said.

"We want to know about Jesus too," said the hotel owner.

Dan looked at his team. "Of course," he said. "We should have spoken to you sooner."

The entire hotel staff gathered in a conference room to listen to one of the team members, Jim Codde, present the gospel. Fifteen of the workers professed faith in Christ, including the owner of the hotel. With those fifteen believers, yet another church was planted—a "hotel church." Clearly God had a vision even greater than planting 40 house churches in one week.

Because they heard what was happening in the city, the hotel staff had wanted to know about Jesus. The team of nationals and short-term missionaries prayed that this movement would continue as the new Burmese churches began reaching out to their countrymen. They prayed that many more Buddhists would hear about the believers' changed lives and want to know what was happening.

The Power to Save

It was a hot, muggy day in Cambodia. The village was quiet, and the everyday work and business of the people was a mere hum in the background. But there was one place in the village where something out of the ordinary was happening.

A group of curious townsfolk walked to the house where they had been told to meet. In the front yard, Dan and his team of missionaries were waiting to greet the villagers. The youngest member of their team—a teenage girl named Kendall—stood at Dan's side with a friendly smile on her face. One by one the Cambodians sat down on the grass and prepared themselves to listen to what the Americans had to say.

As Dan stepped out in the middle of their semi-circle, the villagers shaded their eyes against the sun, squinting to look up at him. Dan took a moment to gather his thoughts before he began speaking. These people had never even heard the name of Jesus before. Dan wanted to share the gospel with them, but first they needed context.

"In the beginning, God created the heavens and the earth." Dan quoted the first verse of the Bible. If he was going to start at the beginning, he would need to start at the very beginning.

Dan went through the whole plan of salvation, laid out from the Old to New Testament.

59

He described the fall of man, and how sin had corrupted the world. "No one who has sinned can be in heaven with God," Dan explained, "and we are all sinners. But God doesn't want us to be separated from Him. He loves us."

The villagers watched him patiently, but there was no sign of stirring in their features. They merely listened.

"God sent his Son to take the punishment we owed—death for sins," Dan went on. "Three days later he rose again, and now anyone who trusts in Christ can be cleansed of their sin and can spend eternity in heaven with God. All you have to do is know that you are a sinner and believe that Jesus died for you, and then ask Him to take away your sins and be your Lord."

Dan looked at the villagers sitting on the grass. They were still gazing up at him, still listening.

"Would any of you like to ask Christ to be your Savior?" Dan offered.

The villagers dropped their heads, some turning to look behind them, others quietly conferring with their neighbors. But no one raised their hands.

This was unusual. Usually people were very open and receptive to the gospel. Not that these villagers were hostile, but none of them appeared to accept the gospel message as truth.

Dan's team shifted uncomfortably behind him. Now what should they do?

The Holy Spirit led Dan to ask a different question. "Do any of you have any prayer requests?"

The villagers looked at each other again. Then one of them, a middle-aged woman, raised her hand. She was trembling, and her pale forehead was beaded with sweat.

"I have a terrible fever," she said hoarsely. "And my head is full of pain. Can you pray for me to be healed?"

Dan smiled and placed his hand on Kendall's shoulder. "Yes. My friend, Kendall, will pray for you."

The teenage girl glanced up at him questioningly. Dan nudged her forwards, nodding to the sick woman. Silently, Kendall said a prayer for her words to be guided by God and then walked out into the crowd of villagers.

Kendall knelt beside the sick woman. The woman was very weak; the fever had clearly ravaged her body. Taking a deep breath, Kendall laid her hands on the woman's head. "Lord, heal this woman in Your name, for Your glory," Kendall prayed. "Remove the sickness from her body and take away the fever that is causing her pain. In Jesus' name, Amen."

Slowly, Kendall took her hands away from the woman's temples. The woman shakily reached up to her head and touched it. Then she turned towards Kendall, staring in shock. "I feel no pain," the woman whispered.

The woman's friends gathered around her, eyes wide, talking in hushed voices. The woman who had been healed carefully stood up, grasping onto Kendall's arm. She found Dan's eyes. "This Jesus is God," she said firmly. "What you have said is truth."

The other villagers also stood, turning towards the group of missionaries. Their faces showed awe, realization, and desire.

"I want to accept Jesus as my Savior," the woman said. Kendall began trembling herself as she held onto the woman's arm.

"So do I." One of the woman's friends stepped up beside her. Soon eight others had joined them, and the missionaries went and knelt with each one. As the missionaries led them in prayer, the ten Cambodians trusted Christ and were saved.

    Kendall prayed again with the woman, this time for the healing of her soul. When the woman finished praying, her face was alight with joy. She embraced Kendall fiercely. Kendall wrapped her arms around the woman's shoulders, and as she did so, she began crying. She hugged the woman tighter. God had brought this woman into His eternal Kingdom and had saved another precious, precious life from death.

The Face of Jesus

E3 Partners, while working in India, decided to adopt the Meiteis as an unreached people group. Teams regularly traveled to India to minister among the Meiteis and to partner with the local believers. One of the staff involved in this effort was a pastor named Joe. Joe had started working with e3 Partners after going on a mission trip with Dan to Lithuania. During that trip, Joe saw how hungry people were for the gospel and what amazing things God was doing through the nationals, and his heart was transformed.

"We've been doing it all wrong," Joe had said, completely shaken. He had seen how inward-focused he and his church and his nation were. During that short trip, a passion for missions and God's glory in the nations consumed him. Joe wanted to resign as a pastor and go out into the mission field full-time. But instead God told him, "Go back to your church, and turn it into a missions sending-center."

So Joe returned home to his church in San Diego, and told the congregation, "There is a world out there, and we need to reach them—both locally and internationally." Joe began leading his church to become involved in missions and to be nations-focused, and he, himself, started working part-time with e3 Partners.

While e3 Partners' work among the Meiteis in India was ongoing, Joe's wife, Tricia, was invited to Bangladesh to speak at a missionary women's retreat. There, she spent some time touring the area. She was taken to the outlying villages and compounds, where the people were mostly Hindu.

As they passed one compound, Tricia peered closely at it. "That looks just like a Meitei compound," she said, puzzled. The Meiteis arranged their family compounds in a way different from any other people group.

"Oh yeah," her guide said. "These are Meiteis."

Tricia was excited. She carried the news back to e3 Partners and her church, New Hope. Because they had adopted the Meteis, they decided that wherever the Meiteis were found, e3 Partners and New Hope Church would raise up teams to go there and work. Accordingly, they began sending teams to Bangladesh.

On their third trip to Bangladesh, of which Joe was a part, the team took along a man named Luxon. Luxon was a Meitei leader who lived in India. He was a wise, charismatic, bold spiritual leader, with a passion for God and His glory. Many at e3 Partners had been praying that God would call Luxon to be a missionary to the Meiteis in Bangladesh. He was the man that had been on all their hearts as they asked God for someone to further the work in India. So, as the team ministered in Bangladesh with Luxon, they were all praying that Luxon would be moved to become involved long-term.

Luxon prayed about the situation fervently and seriously. He desired to reach out to these Meitei villages, and he knew his friends were praying desperately for him to accept the position as missionary. But he needed to be sure that this was what God wanted.

"Please, Lord," he prayed, "Show me what I am supposed to do."

One morning, Joe, Tricia, and another team member were sitting in a room, praying. They were praying specifically for Luxon. As Joe finished his prayer, the door to the room opened. Luxon walked in, and his eyes met Joe's. Instantly, Luxon started beaming. Joe looked at Luxon wonderingly. Luxon's eyes were sparkling, and there seemed to have passed over him a great peace and confidence. Everyone could tell that something had happened in that moment.

"What's up?" Joe asked, walking towards Luxon.

Luxon grinned at Joe. "I was asking God what I should do. I said, 'If the first person I see when I walk into this room is Joe—then I'll know that this is what You want.' And you were the first person I saw."

Everyone rejoiced at the news. They knew God would use Luxon in amazing ways here in Bangladesh.

The next morning, Joe and Luxon were planning to visit one of the outlying villages. Luxon had been there earlier and had witnessed some openness to the gospel. Luxon thought if they went back, there would be people willing to listen to what they had to say.

Over breakfast that day, before they headed out, Joe asked Luxon about his family. Luxon's family members were all strong, bold believers.

"How did you become Christians?" Joe asked.

Luxon told him the story of how his parents had heard the gospel and turned from their Hindu gods to follow Christ. "Afterwards, my father became very vocal in his faith," Luxon said. "He would record the gospel on tapes and send them to the Philippines. From there, the tapes would be broadcasted around the world."

Well, that's cool, Joe thought.

After breakfast, Joe and Luxon drove away from the city and out into the more remote regions. The trip took them a few hours, but at last they arrived at one of the Meitei compounds. Luxon led the way to the house of a man whom he had met on his first visit. At the house, Luxon and the man began a deep conversation.

Joe sat back, watching. Luxon was a brilliant communicator. He answered all of the man's questions with a calm, loving demeanor, and presented the gospel clearly and powerfully. As time passed, and the two men's conversation continued, Joe blinked drowsily. The man's house was nice, and the chair he was sitting in was comfortable. From outside, warm, liquid sunlight spilled onto his shoulders, and a sweet, gentle breeze wafted past his face.

The lure of the outdoors was inviting. And if he sat here any longer, Joe thought he might fall asleep. Quietly excusing himself, Joe slipped from the house, leaving Luxon and the man talking intensely.

Joe walked slowly through the compound, looking for someone he could talk to. A short distance away, an old man was sitting in a chair, his eyes half-closed. As Joe approached, the old man opened his eyes and smiled pleasantly.

"Hello," Joe introduced himself. "My name is Joe. I'm here with my friend Luxon."

The old man sat up, nodding his head. "Yes, I remember seeing him. It's good to meet you."

They started talking. Joe was praying for an opportunity to share the gospel with the man, but as they talked, Joe found out that he was already a Christian.

"I was saved 30 years ago," the man said, in response to Joe's amazed inquiry. "I've never met another believer. I'm the only Christian here."

"How did you hear the gospel?" Joe asked.

"There was this broadcast," the man said, wrinkling his brow as if remembering some distant thought, "a broadcast from the Philippines. A man shared the gospel and how to be saved, and I decided to follow Jesus."

Joe stared at the old man, shocked. "This is amazing," Joe said in a hushed tone. "Would you believe who I have with me today? Luxon is the son of the very man who spoke in the broadcast."

The man's eyes grew wide.

Joe could hardly believe it. Here, this very morning, he had found out about Luxon's father broadcasting the gospel around the world. And now, here Joe was speaking with a man who—30 years before—had been saved by one of those same broadcasts. Of all the villages around the world, God had brought Luxon to this one, where his father had led a man to Christ.

"I have believed in Jesus for 30 years," the old man said tearfully. "I trust in Him. But I want to know more. I haven't heard anything more about him since that broadcast. All these years I have been searching, wanting to see the face of Jesus."

Joe smiled. He pulled his EvangeCube out of his pocket and opened it to the panel of Jesus on the cross. The man stared at the picture of his Lord, his eyes quivering with tears.

"I'm here to share with you the face of Jesus," Joe said softly.

The old man began to smile, taking in every detail of the image. "My Jesus," he whispered.

Joe showed the man all the panels of the cube, from Jesus' death to his resurrection from the grave. He told the faithful old man about the Lord whom he had been serving for 30 years, without knowing anything more than what he had heard in the broadcast from Luxon's father.

Luxon was overjoyed and awed when Joe told him the story. He thanked God for allowing him to see the fruit of his family's work in this old man's life.

As God led him, Luxon did indeed become a full-time missionary to the Meiteis in Bangladesh. He moved to the area and began ministering there, and is still continuing, even now.

Somebody Town

Dan Hitzhusen and his team of short-term missionaries listened attentively as the Ethiopian national began his story:

Bekele was a 70-year-old Ethiopian missionary. One day, he felt God leading him to go to a town called Somebody Town. The old man responded to the command and journeyed to Somebody Town, where he began to share the gospel.

But the people there didn't want to hear what Bekele had to say. Somebody Town was strongly Muslim. When Bekele came to their town speaking of Jesus and salvation, the Muslims angrily attacked him. Bekele was beaten severely and thrown out of Somebody Town.

Bekele lay on the side of the road, unconscious. The Muslims had left him for dead and gone back to Somebody Town. The road was quiet. No one was around. As the ever-blazing sun beat down on the old man's slumped body, it seemed that Bekele would be left to the birds and the parching heat.

Then a young man came driving down the road. His car was old and dusty and it rattled loudly as it bounced over the rutted, rocky roads. The young man had his eyes fixed on the road, trying to navigate the pot-holes. He drove up towards the place where Bekele lay.

Screech! The young man slammed on his brakes, sucking in a sharp breath as he saw the old man, lying bloody and bruised in the dirt.

He scrambled out of his car and slammed the door behind him, running towards Bekele. "Sir!" he called anxiously. "Sir, are you alright?"

Bekele made no response. The young man knelt beside Bekele, his brow furrowed with worry as he examined the old man's injuries. "You need to be at a hospital," the young man said softly.

"Come on." He slipped his arm under Bekele's shoulders, and with a grunt of exertion he lifted the old man from the ground. Carefully, trying not to hurt Bekele any further, he lowered him into the car. "I'll get you help," the young man promised, making Bekele comfortable. "You'll be alright."

Bekele lay lifeless, his face pale and blank.

The young man was a Christian. He drove Bekele to the hospital as quickly as he could and left the old man in the care of the doctors. Bekele's family was notified about what had happened. They quickly came and attended him, and the old man was given the best treatment the hospital could provide.

But Bekele wouldn't wake up. After several days, the doctors informed the family that he was in a coma. There was no telling when, or if, he would ever come out of it.

A month went by. During that time Bekele's family waited on him faithfully, and his church kept him in constant prayer, but Bekele didn't awaken. His wounds had long since healed, but his mind still lay dormant.

Then, in the early morning nearly three months after he had been attacked,

Bekele's eyelids fluttered. Immediately the hospital staff was all around, monitoring him. Bekele took in a long, slow breath, his eyes still closed. He exhaled, and his chest began to rise and fall normally again. His shallow breaths deepened, his fingers began to twitch, and gradually, Bekele opened his eyes.

Bekele began to recover. He quickly regained his wiry strength, suffering no loss of faculty from his ordeal. He began attending his church again. The believers warmly welcomed him back, commenting on his great recovery.

"We're glad you are back safely," one of them said. "Somebody Town is much too dangerous."

Bekele looked surprised. "Oh, I haven't stopped working in Somebody Town. I'm just here until I get better. Then I'm going back to Somebody Town to start a church."

The congregation shook their heads, frowning. "Are you crazy?" they asked. "Those people tried to kill you! You can't go back there."

Bekele raised his chin stubbornly. "They need to know Jesus. God told me to go tell them about Him."

"You are old! You should retire," they said.

"If you can show me in the Bible when Paul retired, or when Peter retired," Bekele said, with a slight smile, "Then I will retire."

The congregation began to mumble and mutter. They couldn't show Bekele anything like that in the Bible. But they still insisted that he not return to Somebody Town.

Eventually, Bekele gave up trying to convince them. He knew they wouldn't support his mission work, so he went to his family.

"If you would, send your tithe money to support me," he said, "Because I'm going to Somebody Town to preach the gospel."

True to his word Bekele left the church, left his home, and left his family, and went back to Somebody Town. He shared the gospel, and this time a few people did come to Christ—enough to start two churches in the Muslim town.

"So, that is the story of our churches," the national said, smiling.

"Wow," Dan said in awe. "That's amazing." His teammates nodded their agreement.

Because of Bekele's courage and determination, there was a foundation laid in Somebody Town for new work to be done.

A Break in Enemy Lines

Dan and the team from e3 Partners had come to Ethiopia to partner with the two churches that Bekele had planted. They planned to build on Bekele's ministry and help the believers in Somebody Town plant more churches—in an area that was still largely hostile and unreached by the gospel.

But when Dan's team first started planning the trip to Somebody Town, some of the Ethiopian believers who worked in Addis Ababa, the capital, tried to warn them not to come.

"It's too dangerous," they said.

Only several months before, two church buildings had been destroyed in Somebody Town. On the orders of the Muslim sheik (the religious leader) one church had been burned to the ground and the other had had a bomb thrown into it. There had been people inside, and a number were killed by the explosion.

Some of the national missionaries from Somebody Town, whom Dan and the team would be working with, bore injuries from the bombing: one had lost an eye, others had limbs missing. Many had relatives and friends who had been killed. Even so, the missionaries were still trying to reach the very people who had attacked them. They said to Dan and his team, "Please come! God has great things He wants to do."

Dan and the team prayed about what God's will was for them and asked for His wisdom to guide their choices. Afterwards, the team felt God leading them to go to Somebody Town, despite the danger, to partner with the local missionaries.

Sharing the gospel was extremely difficult and dangerous for the Ethiopian missionaries in Somebody Town. In fact, this area of Ethiopia was known as "the graveyard of Ethiopian missionaries." But in the local Muslim culture, there was an honor code towards foreigners—to show them hospitality.

Therefore, it was decided that the first step in establishing a ministry in Somebody Town would be to arrange a meeting with the Muslim sheik. Dan, as the leader of the Americans, would be appropriate in asking to meet with the leader of the Muslims upon entering their area. This was an expression of honor to the sheik and in keeping with the Muslim code of hospitality.

Simply because Dan was not from Ethiopia, he might be able to open some doors which the local missionaries could not.

The missionaries from Somebody Town were excited that the American team was coming to help them, but they were very careful about keeping them safe. When Dan and the team arrived, these local missionaries had them stay at a place six hours away from Somebody Town. They were afraid that if the team was any closer to the town, the Muslims would find out where they were staying and try to harm them.

But the long trip to Somebody Town was a nightmare. The roads were terrible and scored with deep ruts. For six hours the team members were jolted and bounced around in the van, and by the time they made it to the village, it was already afternoon. There was only enough time for Dan and the team to set up the meeting with the sheik for the next day. Then they had to load back into the van for the six hour return trip to their hotel.

After living through that ordeal just once, Dan thought wearily, *These roads are going to kill us before the Muslims do. How can we work in Somebody Town and make this trip every day?*

"Thank you for your caution," Dan said to their hosts. "But could you please find us somewhere closer to stay? We won't be very useful for helping you if we can't even keep our eyes open!" The local missionaries agreed, and the team was moved to a hotel much closer to Somebody Town.

After a short drive the next morning, the team arrived in Somebody Town and met up with the local missionaries. As previously arranged, Dan went to the sheik's house to speak with him. The Muslim leader was polite and friendly. He welcomed Dan, got him something to drink, and then the two of them sat down and talked. This was the man who had ordered the churches burned and bombed, but it would be against his beliefs to be hostile towards his guest.

As they talked, Dan was able to share the gospel using an approach called the "Camel Method." It involved making a bridge from the Quran to the New Testament, by discussing the verses in the Quran which talk about Isa (Jesus) and His connection to God. The sheik was open to talking about the Quran, and when Dan transferred to the gospel, he continued to listen. Dan finished by showing him the EvangeCube and going all the way through the salvation story.

The sheik looked thoughtful as Dan put the EvangeCube away. "One of my wives is a Christian," he said. "She's been talking to me about this..." He nodded slowly. "I might be able to see myself becoming a Christian someday."

"Would you be willing to stop attacking the Christians here in Somebody Town?" Dan asked. This was the big question. The entire team of Americans and local missionaries had prayed that Dan's conversation with the sheik would convince him to stop fighting against their outreach. If the sheik agreed, the local missionaries could begin working in ways that they hadn't been able to before.

The sheik considered for a moment, while Dan held his breath and silently prayed.

"Yes, I agree," the sheik said resolutely. "I will not destroy any more churches, and I will stop killing the Christians."

Dan smiled in relief. "Thank you, Sheik," he said. While the sheik was entertaining Dan, that question had hung in the balance. But now the sheik had promised he wouldn't hurt the Christians—which, of course, included Dan himself.

The believers praised God when they heard the news.

The local missionaries had not been able to plant many churches in this part of Ethiopia because of the fierce opposition from the local Muslim leader. But because of the Muslim code of honor, the team had been given the chance to make peace between the sheik and the Christians in Somebody Town. In a strange way, God had used the Americans to break through the "enemy lines," clearing the way for the faithful nationals to spread the Good News of Jesus Christ.

Let's Just Play

It was trading day in Somebody Town.

The town was packed with people; nearly a thousand donkeys, loaded with wares, were being led down the streets. Everyone from the surrounding villages had come to Somebody Town to buy and sell.

Dan, the team, and their interpreters were walking through the village, gazing at all the flurry and bustle around them. Then, to his right, Dan saw a group of young Muslim Ethiopian men—playing volleyball. Their court was merely lines drawn in the dirt and a ragged net suspended from two poles in the middle. The teams hit an old, battered ball back-and-forth.

Riveted, Dan stopped walking and watched the game. He loved playing volleyball. In fact, because he lived near the beach in California, Dan played volleyball all the time. As the young men hit the ball back and forth, calling out to their teammates, Dan started itching to get involved in the game.

A couple of the young men noticed Dan and his team standing nearby. One of the players shouted at Dan, followed by several yells from his teammates.

Dan turned to his interpreter. "I want to play volleyball," he said.

The interpreter looked at him, eyes wide. "No, you don't," he said, shaking his head vigor-

71

ously.

"But...I want to play volleyball," Dan repeated.

"No, you don't," the interpreter said emphatically.

Dan tilted his head. "I do want to play volleyball," he said again.

The interpreter gestured towards the young men on the court. "Do you know what they just said? They called you a 'white devil' and told you to get out of their town."

Dan hesitated, looking from the interpreter to the volleyball court and back again. Despite the meeting with the sheik, he had no guarantee that he would be safe among this huge crowd of Muslim villagers.

"I still want to play volleyball," he said.

The interpreter gave up.

Dan walked over to the volleyball court. The guys eyed Dan warily as he approached, wondering why he was hanging around. Smiling at them, Dan picked one of the teams and walked on to the court. The Ethiopian men exchanged glances. What were they supposed to do? This man didn't seem to care that they didn't want him around.

Dan politely ignored their silent deliberations, simply waiting for the game to resume. Eventually one of the young men tossed the ball back into the air. The serve was to Dan's team. One of the players hit it towards the net, but it was going to fall short. Dan leapt up and struck the ball again, sending it to one of his teammates who hit it over the net towards the other side. The opposing team barely saved it. Their players got a few more volleys in before the ball fell to the ground, earning Dan's team a point.

Dan cheered and gave the player who had hit the ball a high five. The Ethiopian looked at Dan uncertainly, a hint of respect in his eyes. He turned towards his teammates, but they only murmured noncommittally.

The other team hit the ball high into the air and the players scrambled to their positions. They squinted up at the sun, straining to see where the ball was. Then the young man at the corner caught it with a light upward hit, and from there it fell towards a man at the middle.

The player saw Dan waiting near the net. Without hesitating, he passed the ball to Dan, who spiked it over the net and down into the other team's court. This time, the young men returned Dan's high-fives with broad smiles.

As he congratulated his teammates, Dan took a good look around him for the first time since the game had begun.

Oh dear, Dan thought.

The volleyball court was now surrounded by people. There were literally a thousand spectators pressing up to the lines, crowding and squeezing to get a better view. Everyone wanted to watch the 'white devil' play volleyball.

Dan turned a full circle, beginning to feel uneasy. There were villagers ringing him in on every side. Here he was, the only American, completely alone in the midst of hundreds of Ethiopian Muslims. He couldn't see anything over the heads of the huge throng. He had no idea where his team was. And his interpreter...well, how could he find his Ethiopian interpreter in this kind of crowd?

All he could really do was keep playing volleyball.

Dan's team received the ball again. The ball was served, sailing upwards and melding into the sunlight for one moment before plummeting down to earth. Dan saw it heading towards the edge of the court, and he made a dive, getting his fists under the ball before it hit the ground. He passed it to one of the young men, who hit it to a player at the net. The player struck it over the net, where the other team caught it and volleyed it between them.

Dan jumped to his feet, covered in dust and grinning. One of his teammates scored another point and the surrounding crowd erupted in cheers of delight. Dan shouted and clapped with the rest of his team, the young men laughing and slapping him on the back. There were smiles everywhere. Dan grinned. It was stiflingly hot and he was sweating and panting, but he didn't care.

Dan's team received the ball again, and one of them hit it over the net with a hard, sharp strike. The other team ran for it, but they were going to be too late—it was going to hit the ground at the edge of the court—bam! From out of nowhere, one of Dan's teammates leapt from the crowd and dove towards the ball, hitting it up into the air just a moment before it touched the ground. The crowd went wild. They yelled and shouted and screamed as Dan's friend, David, moved onto the court with the other team. The team grinned at David, and he nodded to them, beaming.

"If that's how you want it," Dan called to David, hiding a smile.

David feigned an aggressive stance. "Let's play," he shouted back.

The two teams battled it out in the hot Ethiopian sun, while the crowd continued to press in around the court. Soon the people got so close to the players that the teams were running out of room on the court, and someone had to actually beat the audience off the line with a stick. The people didn't seem to mind.

When the game was finally over, both teams congratulated each other. The spectators kept clapping and clapping, their trading long forgotten. Dan felt a glow inside him as he shook hands with the young men, all shining with sweat and smiling hugely.

All of these people knew that Dan and his friends were Christians. Now they knew that they were fun and friendly and good volleyball players too—and for the moment, that was enough. This was not a time to preach. This was simply a time for the American Christians and the Ethiopian Muslims to play volleyball together.

The atmosphere in Somebody Town was beginning to shift. There was now an opening for the local Ethiopian believers to expand their ministry. Within the next four years, the national missionaries in this area would plant over 150 churches.

You Look Like Jesus

Two years ago, when she was 21 years old, Amber had gone on her first mission trip with e3 Partners. Her team had traveled to Rwanda, where Amber had had the privilege of sharing the gospel in a particular area. The people who heard her message had accepted Christ as their Savior, and the new believers had started a church in their community. Two years later, Amber was on staff with e3 Partners and was leading her first team to Rwanda with Dan Hitzhusen.

When the team arrived in Rwanda, they went to visit the church that Amber had been able to help start on her last trip to the area. There were now fifty people in attendance, the numbers having swelled since Amber was there. The congregation welcomed Amber and her team enthusiastically. They remembered how Amber had first brought them the Good News of Jesus and had told them how they could be saved. At 8 a.m. the service began, and the team celebrated and praised God with the congregation, lifting their loud, joyous worship up to heaven.

During the service, the church presented Amber with a plaque thanking her for being a part of forming the church two years before. Amber accepted the gift with tears in her eyes. She couldn't believe that God had allowed her to be involved in something like this—seeing a church planted which was continuing to be faithful and grow, even beyond its own walls.

At 9 a.m., the team went to the church which that first church had started. There were over a hundred people there and the team enjoyed another time of worship with them. Then Amber and Dan and a few other team members got up and spoke, sharing a brief message and testimony with the congregation. It was amazing to see the healthy, thriving church that had grown from the outreach of the first church. And still, the outreach was continuing.

At 10 a.m., the team went to a third church, which the second church had started—their daughter church and a granddaughter church to the first church! This congregation was composed of about 50 people, and it was also growing strongly and rapidly. Just by sharing the gospel, Amber had been part of starting a church planting movement, which had multiplied to the third generation in only two years. It was an incredible blessing to be able to see the results of how God had used Amber to spread His glory.

On this return trip to Rwanda, Amber's team was partnering with 12 local churches to try to start 12 new churches within the week. The 20 Americans and 320 Rwandans all split up into smaller teams, and each group went out into a different area to share the gospel.

Dan and Amber went out with several interpreters and a group from the local church. When they arrived in the town where they would be working, they began going from house-to-house and talking with the people, making friends and sharing the gospel.

Their group was walking down a road through town, traveling to the next house, when a man walked up to them from across the street. He strode straight up to Dan and looked him right in the eye.

"You look like Jesus," he said abruptly.

Dan was taken aback. He glanced at his teammates, not sure what to think. What was this man talking about?

"I want to tell you," the man continued, keeping his gaze fixed firmly on Dan. "You can have my wife, my children, my grandchildren—but you can't have me."

They began talking with the man, and found out that he had had a vision of premonition before they arrived. Somehow, he had known they were coming, and he had known that they were bringing news of Jesus.

After speaking with them for a while, the man invited the team to come to his home and have something to eat. The team looked quickly at each other. An invitation to their home was one of the marks of a "person of peace"—someone who would be the center of ministry in a new area. E3 Partners' teams looked for such a person in every area where they ministered, as Jesus had taught in Luke, chapter 10.

The team followed the man to his house, where his wife graciously set out some food. They met his children and his grandchildren as well. As they ate and visited with the family, Dan told the man the story of salvation and how Jesus wants everyone to come to repentance and have eternal life.

"If you believe that Jesus died for your sins and accept Him as your Savior and Lord, you will be saved," Dan explained.

The man was quiet for a moment. He looked at Dan and then up at his wife and children. Then he bowed his head in submission. "Jesus may have me," he said softly. "I want Him to be my Savior."

The team prayed with him—and with his wife, children, and grandchildren as well. Jesus received all of them into His kingdom that day.

Because he was a "person of peace," the team began to concentrate their ministry on this man's community. Many of his friends and neighbors came to Christ, until several hundred people in that area had professed faith in Christ. Soon the believers had gathered to start a church. The man had a cornfield behind his house, and he offered that area as the site for a meeting house. He provided timber for the walls, and some Burundi pastors—who were working with the team—provided funds for a tin roof. The building was erected in the backyard of this man, the "person of peace," and a new church was born by the grace of God.

Forgiven

During the week that Amber, Dan and their team were in Rwanda, 340 people were out sharing the gospel, and in every area where the believers traveled, many people came to Christ and many churches were started. The Rwandans were extremely open to the gospel. The story of forgiveness and new life resonated deeply with them.

But what was the reason for this huge reception of the gospel? Why were the people of Rwanda so desperate for salvation?

The team had arrived in Rwanda in the shattered aftermath of the genocide that had taken place across the country. For three months, a satanic possession had come over the people and they had committed terrible crimes against each other. Neighbors attacked neighbors, people were slaughtered, and horrific, brutal murders were carried out against innocents.

After a period of hellish carnage, the Rwandan people suddenly woke up. Without knowing how it had happened, they found themselves with blood on their hands and their entire country in screaming shambles around them. They had done things they never, ever thought they would do. They had committed deeds that would haunt them for the rest of their lives.

The president of Rwanda, a Christian, knew that if they prosecuted every person who had been involved in the massacres, they would be unable to complete the courts within their lifetimes and the arrests would bankrupt their society—there would be no people left. So the country arranged to prosecute the top 300 criminals and to hold genocide courts for everyone else.

Every Tuesday at a set time of day, the towns shut down and everyone halted their labor. Then the people would gather at a local outdoor court. Every week it was the same. Every week for as long as it would take, another genocide court would be held to try to bring redemption to this broken land.

On one particular Tuesday, the court was full yet again. These were all people who knew each other; some had grown up together, others were close friends, others were close neighbors. They all sat silently, wondering what crimes would be spoken that day and who would confess them.

Two men stood up. Slowly, their legs trembling beneath them, they walked up to the front and stood before the judge. The judge nodded for them to begin.

Swallowing hard, the first man spoke. "I-I was the one who murdered your family," he whispered, fixing his gaze on his neighbor who was sitting alone in the audience. His neighbor looked fixedly at him, a single tear sliding down his cheeks.

"We both," the man gestured to the younger one beside him, "We both came in the night and killed them. And I—" he broke off, his shoulders beginning to shake. "I am so…so sorry—"

The courtroom was hushed as the man wept. The neighbor, too, was crying freely now, grieving for his family and for his friend.

"What does the court say?" The judge asked, gazing around the room.

There was a rustle among the seats and a few whispers. Then the crowd said as one voice, "Forgiven."

The two men looked up, their eyes glowing with hope and their faces shining with tears.

"Forgiven," his neighbor whispered.

The two men would be assigned a service to perform for the community. And the next Tuesday, another person would step forward—maybe it would be the neighbor. But even as the people found out who had killed their families or murdered their friends, their call was almost always the same: "Forgiven." Most people didn't seek revenge. They didn't hurt the people who had confessed or their families. Almost everyone had been a part of the genocide. Almost everyone was guilty. And everyone wanted it to end.

As a result of these genocide courts, the Rwandan people already had a powerful image of sin and forgiveness, and mercy for guilty people. So when the believers came sharing the gospel, the Rwandans didn't just hear the story of salvation—they felt it. They longed for it from the bottom of their hearts. They had felt the release of forgiveness by men. But what would it be like to truly have new life—to be forgiven by God?

The team of 340 believers was working in a mountainous region where there had been many rebel strongholds. The people who lived there had some of the greatest burdens to carry. They had committed a large number of the most horrible crimes, and as a result, they were some of the people most open to the gospel.

The believers had the privilege of bearing Jesus' message of hope and grace to these people. But it was God's Spirit working in the despairing hearts and souls of the people of Rwanda that caused them to respond in such massive numbers. During the week that Amber, Dan, and their team were in Rwanda—during the time that the 340 believers were out sharing the gospel—5,345 people professed faith in Christ.

The Future in His Hands

"You plant a church—in a week," Rick said skeptically.

Dan grinned. "You want to come with us next trip? You can see firsthand how God does it."

"I'll think about it," Rick said.

While Rick was thinking about it, a national missionary from Slovenia had come to the United States asking for help in his ministry, and in response, e3 Partners had asked Dan to lead a team to Slovenia. Dan's invitation for team members was simple: "If you can fog a mirror, you can come!" The collection of people he acquired was a rag-tag bunch, but they were all enthusiastic and willing. Then Dan told Rick about the trip and was able to convince him to come along as well.

A short while later, Dan and Rick and a motley team of short-term missionaries were flying to Slovenia, a small country directly beneath Austria.

The team traveled to the capital of Slovenia, a city called Ljubljana. That first night they went to a church service where Rick, who was a pastor, preached the gospel message. He asked if anyone wanted to accept Christ.

Two people raised their hands. But both of the hands belonged to members of Rick's own

79

team! At that point Rick felt a little discouraged. Yes, he was glad that the two team members, who were originally from Slovenia and had been taught a different doctrine of salvation, had come to Christ. But he hadn't expected to find out that some of his own team members weren't saved! And none of the others had responded to the message that night.

But after the service was over, a woman came up to Dan and Rick. She was thrilled to meet the Americans. "I know some of you are coming to my city tomorrow," she said excitedly, "and it's a long drive. I would love for your team to stay at my house tonight."

Dan thought the situation over. He wasn't going with the team to this woman's city. The Americans were splitting up between two different cities. Dan was traveling to one place, and a new e3 Partners missionary named Craig Poston was leading the other team. Dan didn't know anything about this woman—who she was or where she lived. Should he send part of his team off with her?

Dan prayed his customary prayer for wisdom. Then he thought, "Why not?"

"Guys, this woman has offered to take you in for the night," Dan told his team. "She's extremely pleased to have you stay with her."

Craig and a few of the team gathered their belongings and followed the woman out of the church. Dan watched them go, wondering what adventure awaited them.

The next evening, both teams regrouped. Craig's team found Dan immediately.

"Guess who you sent us with?" one of them said. "She was a Muslim fortune-teller."

Uneasy, Dan waited for the rest of the story, wondering what had happened.

"She tells the future by reading tea leaves, with the help of an evil spirit," Craig went on to explain. "We spent the night at her house, and in the morning got to talking." He started to smile, and another team member quickly picked up the story.

"We shared the gospel with her over breakfast," he said eagerly. "And she came to Christ! Then we told her the story, you know, about Lydia at the river? How when Paul came and shared the gospel with her, she responded to his message and then asked him to come and stay at her house."

"We thanked our hostess for asking us to stay with her—and we called her Mama Lydia," the missionary said. "You have to meet her. Because of her occupation, she knows almost everyone in town. She wants to help us share the gospel."

"That's great!" Dan said heartily, inwardly feeling relieved. Apparently his decision to send the team off in the middle of the night with a complete stranger hadn't been a wrong one.

Dan and the rest of the team went to Mama Lydia's city and preached the gospel. In the time they were there, 21 people came to Christ. But out of the 21 people, only two were saved because of the public outreaches Craig's team had set up. Nineteen people accepted Christ because of their relationships with Mama Lydia. Within a week, a new church had been started—a church meeting in Mama Lydia's house. Dan realized that this woman, a Muslim fortune-teller, was their "person of peace." And Rick, completely undone, watched God start a church in one week.

Rick understood now. He was seeing firsthand stories of salvation like those Dan had told him about, and he realized the importance of bringing the knowledge of Christ to the nations. So many people had never even heard the gospel because no one had ever come to tell them. Here in Slovenia, Rick had seen God's power moving in the people's hearts and preparing them to hear the gospel. He had felt the privilege and the excitement of being involved in God's work, doing something that mattered for eternity. And he knew that what he had experienced during this trip was something he wanted to be a part of for the rest of his life.

At the end of the trip, the missionaries had a closing rally which brought together all the people God had touched that week. Mama Lydia came, as well as the new Christians from her city. In front of her family of believers, Mama Lydia told a story of what had happened to her.

"After I accepted Christ, people kept coming to my house, asking me to read their fortunes," she said. "But I told them I was a believer now, and couldn't do that anymore. But these particular people kept asking and asking, and finally…I relented. I threw down the tea leaves which I had used for so many years. But—I couldn't read anything in them anymore." Mama Lydia gazed around the room, smiling peacefully. "The evil spirits that had predicted the future were gone from me. Jesus lives in my heart now."

Mama Lydia looked up at the missionaries who had brought her the gospel, her eyes steady and intense. "God is the only one who can tell the future," she declared, "and I know He holds it in His hands."

Short-term missions that matter

If planned carelessly, short-term mission trips can be a disaster. But build them around a long-term strategy and you'll transform entire communities.

Today, e3 Partners is launching an average of 20 healthy churches every day that are transforming the communities around them. We send thousands of Christians on short-term expeditions to over 40 countries. Each mission trip carefully supports an ongoing field strategy that involves sharing the Gospel, establishing churches, and seeking restoration in unreached communities.

This is intentional, life-changing, get-your-hands-dirty missions that makes a lasting impact.

www.e3partners.org

e3 **PARTNERS**
equip. evangelize. establish.

You Have Not Because You Ask Not

Dan and Rick had arrived in Addis Ababa, Ethiopia. That night there was a church meeting in Arba Minch, with over a thousand Ethiopian Christians gathering to hear them speak. Dan and Rick and the team were waiting at the airport to fly to a city called Awassa and then fly on to Arba Minch. But it didn't look like they would be leaving the airport anytime soon.

Heavy rain and thunderstorms were making it unsafe to fly into Awassa. Even though Arba Minch had good weather, they couldn't get there because the plane had to fly to the connecting city before continuing on.

Dan and Rick sat in the airport waiting for the weather in Awassa to clear and for the announcement to begin boarding the plane. But time continued to tick past without any word. Dan checked his watch, blowing out a nervous breath. The plane still had to fly to Awassa, land, and take off again before they would be actually heading to their destination.

Dan waited a few more minutes and then said plainly, "Rick, we're gonna miss this meeting."

Rick sighed. "I know. But what can we do?"

In response, Dan bowed his head and began to pray. Rick followed suit. They both asked God for a way to get them to the church meeting on time so that they could share their message with the Christians who would be coming.

Then Dan got to his feet. "Let's go up to the desk."

Rick frowned, but he stood up to accompany Dan. "What are you going to ask?"

"If they can divert the plane from Awassa," Dan said, beginning to walk away.

Rick shot out a hand and grabbed him by the arm. "Are you crazy?" Rick exclaimed, pulling Dan back. "You're going to embarrass us. They'll never do something like that."

Dan slipped out of Rick's grip. "Rick, we serve a great God," he said with a smile. "And we'll never know unless we ask." He kept walking towards the desk. Rick looked around helplessly for a moment, and then hurried off after Dan, muttering something under his breath.

"Hello," Dan was saying to the clerk as Rick trotted up, "I'd like to speak to your supervisor."

"What do you need?" the girl asked.

Rick opened his mouth to speak, but Dan got in first. "I want to ask him if the plane could fly straight to Arba Minch without stopping in Awassa."

The girl stared at him, and Rick took the opportunity to jump in. "He's joking," Rick said quickly. "He doesn't really mean—"

"No," Dan said calmly. "I'm not joking. Could I please speak to your supervisor?"

Rick glanced heavenwards and resisted the urge to drag Dan away from the desk—as though it would have done any good.

"Sure, I can get him," the girl said uncertainly. She walked away, casting odd looks at Dan and Rick.

They waited by the desk for her return. Rick swallowed uncomfortably, folding his arms and trying to avoid the gazes of the people looking curiously at them. Dan was oblivious. He bounced impatiently on his toes as he watched for the supervisor to come walking out.

Finally the girl came back with a skinny, rather short man dressed in a black suit. He listened to Dan's story about their need to speak at a special church service in Arba Minch. But, as Rick had expected, he gave no indication that he was planning to cancel the scheduled stop. When he bid Dan and Rick farewell, they could do nothing but return to their seats.

Rick knew Dan's plan had failed. Of course the airline wouldn't change a plane's route just to suit a couple of passengers! Surely now Dan would see what a half-baked idea that had been. But Dan merely bowed his head and began to pray again. "Lord, allow us to get to Arba Minch on time. Please cause the plane to fly straight to Arba Minch, because there is no way we will get to that meeting if it stops in Awassa."

Rick stifled a groan. *Lord*, he prayed, only half-jokingly, *please get me out of here!*

Finally, *finally*, they were allowed to board the flight to Awassa. Rick had resigned himself to missing the meeting—it was simply impossible for them to get there. But Dan remained in stubborn silence as they walked down the narrow chute and climbed into the airplane. Even when they were in their seats and had their seatbelts fastened, he was unwilling to give up.

Dan, Rick wanted to say, *we're already on the airplane. Nothing's going to change now!*

But all he did was sigh softly and glance out the window at the rain-swept runway.

A few minutes later they felt the plane's engine rumble, and the huge vehicle started to roll out onto the take-off strip.

Then the intercom crackled to life. "Ladies and gentlemen, welcome aboard," it announced happily. "We have an important announcement. This plane will not be stopping in Awassa."

No. Way. Rick turned towards Dan with a look of utter shock. Dan grinned hugely.

"We will be flying straight to Arba Minch. Have a great flight!" the intercom clicked off with a crackle of static.

"You did not," Rick said flatly.

"Nope," Dan said merrily. "God did."

The plane flew to Arba Minch, and that morning, right on time, Dan, Rick, and the team arrived at their meeting. They preached God's Word to the faithful Christians in Ethiopia, praising God that He even redirects airplane flights to accomplish His will.

Duckling Discipleship

E3 Partners was always looking for ways to make their strategies more effective. They didn't want to just plant churches. They wanted those churches to multiply and start church planting movements—like what had happened in Rwanda.

Part of e3 Partners' new strategy involved getting people to feel a responsibility to share the gospel. When a person accepted Christ, a team member would ask the new believer if they had friends or family who needed to hear the gospel. If the person said "yes," the team would train them to share the gospel using the EvangeCube or other similar tools. Then the team would ask a second question: Would they share the gospel with those people, using the methods they had learned, by the time the team returned the next day? And would they then bring those people to meet the team? The new believers usually answered, "Yes!"

When Rick, who was now on staff with e3 Partners, first heard about this method, he said, as was his custom: "Dan, you're *crazy!*" They were expecting a ten-minute-old believer to go out and share the gospel? Rick knew many adults in America who had *never* shared their faith, and they had been saved for years!

"Rick," Dan said patiently, "All believers have been given the Great Commission. When someone comes to Christ, we teach them to obey what they know, and at that point—all they know is the gospel. So we instruct them to share it."

"But...right after they're saved?" Rick asked, still skeptical.

"Remember the mother duck principle of discipleship?" Dan said with a smile. "Paul told the Corinthians to 'follow me as I follow Christ.' All you have to do to disciple someone is to stay one step ahead of them while following Christ. Like one duckling following another, all following the mother duck. If someone has heard the gospel and accepted it, they know enough to share it with someone else and disciple them in Christ."

Later, when Rick and his wife, Brenda, went on an e3 trip to Ethiopia, they got to see this strategy work firsthand. Every morning Rick and Brenda would drive down the road out into the wilderness to where a national believer would be waiting for them. This man was from a remote village back in the countryside. He was their guide—the one who would take Rick and Brenda to the village and lead them to the houses that they could visit that day.

The first day Rick and Brenda met their guide on the side of the road, he led them down beaten dirt paths to a small community of mud-brick houses. There they were joined by an interpreter. But before Rick and Brenda set out to share the gospel, the guide asked them to come to *his* house. It would be a great honor for him to have Americans visit.

Rick and Brenda stepped inside the house. It had a mud floor and mud walls and was fairly small, but it was tidy and cozy. Their guide's family greeted them warmly and served them home-brewed coffee. Rick and Brenda talked with the family for a while, sharing their testimonies and taking an opportunity to present the gospel. However, their guide didn't seem to be interested in trusting Jesus. He listened politely, but when Rick finished, he merely smiled and asked if they were ready to begin traveling around the village.

The guide stayed with Rick and Brenda all day. At each house where they shared the gospel, he heard the story of salvation told again and again as Rick and Brenda led several of the villagers to Christ. Occasionally, as he spoke, Rick would glance over at the guide. He was always sitting some distance away, up against the wall or in a shadowed corner, staying out of sight. But he was always listening.

At the end of the day Rick, Brenda, their interpreter, and their guide left the last house. They walked through the village on their way back to the road. Suddenly their guide stepped in front of them. "Would you come back to my house?" he said. "I…I want to accept Jesus as my Savior. And I want to do it with my whole family."

Rick smiled. "Yes, we'll come. Of course." They returned to the guide's house and shared the gospel with his family again. Then together, the entire family knelt and prayed to receive Christ as their Lord and Savior.

Rick and Brenda hugged each new believer and prayed that they would continue strongly in their faith. When it was time to leave, the goodbyes were touched with sadness. Their paths in life were so different that most likely Rick and Brenda would never see this family again. Thankfully, they knew they would all be reunited in the end.

Rick and Brenda returned to the hotel, and the next morning they set out for another village. They drove down the road, past the village they had visited the day before, and on to the next location. When they pulled over to the side of the road, whom should they see but their guide from the day before! He waited for them as they climbed out of the car, looking rather awkward and shy.

"I walked from my village," he said. "I was wondering if I could come with you today, when you share the gospel."

Rick studied him, remembering the strategy that e3 Partners had taught. "Yes, you can come," Rick said. "If you are willing to share the gospel yourself, and tell the villagers why you decided to follow Jesus."

The man looked at him, with both nervousness and excitement shining in his eyes.

"We'll teach you," Rick said, starting to walk along the path. "Come on." The man followed Rick's little team back to the village where they would be doing ministry.

There, Rick and his interpreter taught the guide to share the gospel using the EvangeCube. Before long he was sharing with a group of five men, the interpreter standing nearby to help him if he needed it. The guide led the five men to Christ. He had only been a believer for 24 hours, and yet he had already learned to share his faith and had brought five more people into the Kingdom!

"Well, Dan," Rick murmured as he watched the guide rejoicing with the new believers, "You were right again. It really does work."

A Meeting with Mother Teresa

Dan and his team had concluded an amazing week of ministry in Manipur, India. On their way back to America, the team had a layover in Calcutta, the capital of India. While they were there, they planned to visit the Missionaries of Charity orphanage and maybe catch a glimpse of Mother Teresa—a world-renowned believer who cared for the poor in Calcutta.

Before the team had left the States, Dan had filled out a prayer card for the trip. He listed the places where they would be traveling and what they would be doing, so that people could be praying for them and their ministry.

But the blocks of space for each day on the prayer card were terribly small. Dan didn't even attempt to squeeze "Visit Missionaries of Charity orphanage in Calcutta" onto the paper. Instead he wrote, "Meet Mother Teresa," which wasn't quite accurate, but it fit.

Someone had approached him later, holding one of the prayer cards. "It sounds like you're going to meet Mother Teresa personally," he said, frowning. "Did you get an appointment?"

"Uh, no," Dan said. "I just couldn't write the whole explanation on the card."

"You should make sure it says the right thing," the man advised. "So you tell people the truth."

Dan had agreed, but last minute preparations and the flurry of packing and preparing to leave for India completely drove it from his mind. The prayer card remained, "Meet Mother Teresa." So as Dan and the team boarded the plane to India, people were praying for their travels and for their meeting with Mother Teresa—which wasn't in the plans at all!

In Calcutta, the team made their visit to the Missionaries of Charity orphanage. Inside the orphanage it was crowded, dirty, and smelly. There were three or four babies to a crib, and many wore no diapers. Thin and grimy, the children stretched out longing hands towards the newcomers, begging to be embraced. Many of them were deformed.

Though Dan berated himself for it, his first feeling was revulsion. The entire building was filthy. Even the air stunk. He didn't want to touch the children who reached so desperately towards him.

But Tricia and the other mothers on the team went to the children without hesitation. Unreservedly, with smiles on their faces, they hugged and cuddled the little ones, and the children's answering laughter transformed the place. Soon Dan, too, was hugging and loving on the lonely orphans.

It seemed wrong that so many children should be living in such terrible conditions. Why didn't they get better care? Why didn't they have their own crib, a real toilet, or even a bath? Then Dan realized that he was comparing their quality of life with that of his own baby son back in America. Here in India thousands were in great need. The sidewalks were lined with homeless, parentless children; many parents abandoned their babies on the doorstep of the orphanage. To the Missionaries of Charity, another baby in the crib meant another baby who didn't die of exposure or starvation. While Dan was thinking of the conditions of these lives, the nuns were concerned with simply preserving them.

After visiting with the children for a long while, the team went into another room. The atmosphere was solemn and still; here the Missionaries of Charity knelt in prayer and worship. For hours they knelt on cold concrete floors offering up their praises and petitions to God. Dan and his team observed the meeting, hushed by the calming, rhythmic sound of their prayers.

Dan was kneeling on the ground to watch. But after just a few minutes his knees were aching and his legs were stiff and sore. How did the Sisters stand it for so long? He got up slowly and stretched his legs a bit, pacing the length of the back wall.

All at once he felt an urge to go outside. Dan looked over his shoulder; the rest of the team was still sitting quietly, basking in the tranquility of the room. Silently, being careful not to disturb the Sisters' worship, Dan slipped from the room and found his way to the sidewalk outside.

There, being pushed in a wheelchair down the sidewalk, was Mother Teresa. Dan froze in shocked excitement. The old, frail woman was talking with a benefactor. She smiled kindly, nodding her head several times. Dan sidled closer to the little group and eventually inched in place behind the benefactor. He hoped that they would assume he had come with this man on official business.

The man exchanged a few last words with Mother Teresa to which she responded graciously. Then he turned aside, leaving Dan standing face-to-face with the small, wrinkled woman who was one of the world's greatest humanitarians. She looked at Dan with some surprise on her face.

Dan knelt down on the sidewalk so he could see straight into her eyes. Taking her gnarled hands into his own, he said quietly, "Hello, Mother Teresa. My name is Dan. I'm here with my friends on a mission trip." He described the work they were doing in Manipur, and Mother Teresa squeezed his hands tightly.

"God bless you, brother," she said fervently.

Mother Teresa reached out her trembling hands and laid them on Dan's shoulders. She prayed for Dan and for the other missionaries and for the ministry they had done on their trip in India—and for the rest of the work they would do in the future. Dan was deeply moved as he knelt there in the streets of Calcutta hearing Mother Teresa begging God's blessing over him and the work of e3 Partners.

As Dan thanked Mother Teresa, she signed one of her business cards for him. Dan took the card, giddy with delight despite himself.

"Could you sign ten more of these for my friends?" Dan blurted out.

Mother Teresa's eyes twinkled, and she uncapped her pen again.

By now some of Dan's team had emerged from the building. When they saw Dan and recognized who he was talking with, their eyes grew wide and they began chattering excitedly. Dan waved for them to join him. The team members hurried over, lining up to get Mother Teresa's autograph and a chance to talk with her for a few short moments.

Later, Dan wondered which faithful souls had been consulting their mismarked prayer cards that day and passionately praying for the team's meeting with Mother Teresa. In answer to a request the team hadn't even meant to make, God had arranged the appointment for them.

He Saw Me

John grew up with a traditional Christian background. He went to a small American church where they were taught the Bible and sang praise songs. He believed fully in the power and sovereignty of God. But miracles—his church didn't believe that they happened anymore. And John had never personally seen God perform a demonstrative, supernatural act.

But now John was in Ethiopia, on a mission trip with Dan Hitzhusen. He had taken a step of faith to travel so far from home, and God had a plan to increase his faith even more.

"John, you'll take this village," Dan told him before the team went out. "Remember, you have the tools we showed you. They can open up opportunities for you to share the gospel."

John put his EvangeCube in his pack, and also what was called the HOPE cube. This tool had the same unfolding panels as the EvangeCube, but it discussed HIV/AIDS and practical ways to prevent it. When a missionary offered knowledge about this very serious medical issue, the villagers were eager to listen. Then, once the HOPE cube had been shared, they were more open to hear the gospel.

John arrived at the village with a small group of team members, national missionaries, and interpreters. The Ethiopian villagers watched them curiously as they entered the town; many of the people wanted to find out why they had come.

When John explained the reason for their visit, one of the villagers, an older woman, was interested in hearing more. John sat down with the woman and took her through the HOPE cube, remembering how Dan had taught them. "There are ways to prevent HIV," John said. He showed the woman the pictures on the cube. "Much has to do with a clean lifestyle."

The two of them went over every panel, and as John put the cube back in his pack, he pulled out the EvangeCube. "Would you like to hear about Jesus?" he asked.

The woman studied the cube, interested. She had been grateful to learn about the HOPE cube. Whatever else John had to say, it couldn't hurt to listen.

John began with sin. "We are separated from God because of the wrong things we've done and deserve death for our sin. We have no hope of a relationship with God." John unfolded the cube, revealing the graphic of Jesus' death on the cross. "But God sent his own Son to die in our place. Jesus was buried, and rose again after three days." The next panel showed a sealed tomb, and when John folded the cube in half, an image of Jesus emerged from the grave. "He has defeated death. If anyone admits that they are a sinner and asks Jesus to save them, Jesus frees them from the penalty of death. When they die, they will live forever with God."

Now came the time to ask if the woman wanted to accept Jesus as her Savior. John flipped the cube again, taking the woman to the final panel of the salvation story. "Jesus offers this gift freely to anyone who receives Him. Would you like to ask Him to be your Lord and Savior?"

The woman was silent. She stared off into the distance as if she were remembering something. "Last night..." she said softly. "I had a dream."

John didn't understand. Did the woman not want to listen anymore? Was she trying to change the subject? John wasn't sure what to do. But the woman was continuing, more urgently.

"I had a dream that I was lying on the floor of a hospital, beside a coffin." Her face was haunted at the memory. "I was…cold. I was dead. And all the people in the hospital—they kept walking by me, but they wouldn't look at me."

John felt himself drawn in by the woman's words, equally intrigued and horrified. What was this about?

"But then…" The woman paused, her eyes glistening. She shook her head slowly. "*He* came by. He was God, in the form of a man—and he *saw* me. No one else had looked at me. But he saw me." Tears slipped down her cheeks.

Then the woman raised her head and stared into John's eyes. "God told me that someone would come today and talk with me about what I had seen."

John listened numbly, his heart pounding with awe.

"And now, I know." The woman smiled faintly, glistening tears coating her face. "God sent Jesus to bring me from death to life. And God sent you to tell me about Him."

John's mouth was dry. God had told this woman in a dream that John would be coming to the village, before any of the villagers even knew about the visit. It was a miracle, like the miracles in the Bible—the miracles he had never seen before. But John realized that God's power was in no way dormant. Whatever ways there were to reach a lost soul for Himself, God would use them. This time God had allowed John to witness a demonstration of His supernatural power, which was still moving in people's lives to bring His Name glory.

The woman asked Jesus to be her Savior that day. Not only did John have the encouragement and amazement of seeing God's power at work in a miracle, but he had the blessing of kneeling with the Ethiopian woman as she prayed to the God of the universe to cleanse her from her sins by the blood of Jesus. No longer would she have to fear death—because God had looked upon her and seen her.

By the Dark of Night

Rick was holding a training conference in Amhara, Ethiopia. There, he and his team taught over 20 local believers how to effectively plant churches in their area, training them in strategies such as looking for the "person of peace," and leading Bible studies with the six-question strategy. The majority of the nationals who attended the training were farmers; they had not been educated at seminary or Bible school. They loved the Lord and had a heart to serve Him, and that was all they needed.

After the training was completed, one farmer, named Telayneh, began the long walk home to his village. As he walked, his face was troubled. "Lord," he prayed quietly, "These strategies sound good, and I believe you can do them, but—I have no idea how I am going to plant churches in my village."

Telayneh was afraid. The Orthodox sect had a strong hold over the villages in Ethiopia. He knew that there was a lot of hatred for Christians. Just the year before, in the village next to his, a man had attacked seven new believers with an axe. One had been killed; the others had had appendages cut off.

What would happen if Telayneh started openly sharing the gospel in his village? Would his family be attacked and maimed or killed? He shuddered to think of his wife and precious children being put in danger.

"Lord, I need your help," Telayneh prayed as he journeyed down the long road back home.

After a day of traveling, Telayneh arrived back at his hut. His wife greeted him warmly and his kids tackled his knees with shouts of joy at his return. As Telayneh hugged them, he felt a pang of grief and guilt at the risk he was taking. He loved his family so much...but he knew God had called him to reach out to his countrymen. He had to obey.

That night Telayneh sat beside his fire, staring into the coals. His family had gone to bed, but Telayneh couldn't sleep. The excitement of the training, the new information running through his head, his doubts and fears, and his newfound passion all combined to keep him awake and alert. He spent the time, quiet before the fire, to again ask God to work through him and to do His will.

Then screams rose into the night.

Telayneh started up, frowning in confusion. In these villages, houses were not built close together; there was a considerable distance between each hut. In order for the clamor to reach Telayneh's ears with such volume, there had to be something extreme going on very close by.

Telayneh ran to his front door and yanked it open. The chaos instantly grew louder. Wails and shouts and yells of pain were coming from the hut next to his. What could be happening? Telayneh stared out into the night, wondering what he should do. And suddenly, he felt a strong urge to go over to the house. Telayneh looked back at his safe, quiet house, with the warm fire gently settling into ash. Then he grabbed his jacket and went out the door, closing it carefully behind him. God was prompting him to act. Whatever was happening, Telayneh was supposed to be a part of it.

The noise increased as Telayneh came closer. Now he could see the light of his neighbor's fire glowing dully through the doorway. Moving silently, Telayneh slipped through the darkness and approached the house.

Inside, a woman was screaming. Telayneh's heart pounded as he walked up to the doorway. Carefully, he looked around the doorjamb and saw the scene laid out before him.

The woman was thrashing back and forth, screaming in agony and fear. Her family members, their faces pale and strained, were holding her down as best as they could. Standing over the woman was an Orthodox priest. As Telayneh watched, he realized that the priest was trying to cast out a demon from the woman's body. The priest looked worn and uneasy. Again and again he repeated his words, but the woman continued to scream. The Orthodox priest couldn't drive out the demon.

Telayneh stood there, in the doorway, watching. He wasn't sure what to do. The Orthodox priest stepped back. There was sweat on his brow, but all his efforts had availed nothing. The woman shook violently, twisting in the arms of her family members. The family was panicked. If the priest was powerless, what could they do? Their sobs and wails began to join the woman's, as the priest looked helplessly around the room.

"Only Jesus Christ can heal her."

The wails subsided. The priest and the family turned towards the doorway, startled by this new voice.

Telayneh swallowed as all their eyes looked to him. He was unsure how those words had come out of his mouth—he certainly hadn't meant to say them. *Father, I know you're guiding me,* he prayed. *Show me what to do.*

"What are you saying?" the priest barked. Telayneh stepped into the hut, standing straight.

"Would you let me pray for her?" he asked the family. They nodded, so scared and hopeless that they no longer cared how the help came. The priest backed away as Telayneh entered the house and went to the woman. Telayneh laid his hands on her shoulders and began to pray.

"Lord God, Your power is great. Show Your glory and cast the evil spirit out of this woman's body," he declared boldly, "in the Name of Jesus Christ!"

The woman shot upright with a shrieking scream and then fell silent. For a moment she sat, staring straight at the wall, and then she slowly turned to look at her family. She stared at her loved ones as if seeing them for the first time. "Father?" she asked softly, looking at the elderly man standing by her side.

The family gasped with joy. They flung their arms around her, laughing and crying, and stroking her hair with their hands. Telayneh stepped away, not saying a word. He knew the priest was watching him, but in that moment he felt no fear.

After that night, the whole village knew that Telayneh was a believer. They heard about the miraculous healing and saw the woman, at peace again, with their own eyes. They knew that Telayneh had access to the very power of God.

People were afraid to meet Telayneh in public. But by the dark of night, when no one else could see, they began coming to Telayneh's house with their sick and ailing. They asked him to pray for them. Telayneh invited each and every person into his home. He prayed, and God healed the sick supernaturally.

Then Telayneh shared the gospel with his visitors. One by one, in the middle of the night, the villagers accepted Christ as Savior. Before long, there were so many believers that they no longer stayed in secret. They openly proclaimed their faith and began meeting together in a small house—where Telayneh started his first church. Within three years, Telayneh planted ten other churches in neighboring villages, using the training he had received and the guidance God continued to provide.

Keep On in the Lord's Work

Rick worked in a particular part of Ethiopia where the Orthodox sect ruled unwaveringly. Less than one tenth of one percent of the people believed in Jesus. But the local believers with whom e3 Partners worked were passionate to get the gospel out to their countrymen.

When the e3 teams went over to partner with the nationals, the ministry of the nationals was able to advance. The Orthodox leaders were wary of causing trouble for the Americans, for although the Orthodox priests hated the missionaries for teaching another doctrine and for leading their people away from the Ethiopian Orthodox church, America was their ally, and they couldn't openly attack the Americans. Some rocks would be thrown and the foreign missionaries might get a few nasty shouts, but overall the e3 teams would be left alone.

When e3 teams came to Ethiopia, the Americans and the nationals would go from house to house sharing the gospel. The nationals were trained by the visiting teams to be disciplemakers, so that when the Americans left, these local believers could return to the houses where people had been saved and start Bible studies for the new believers. Unfortunately, when the Americans left, the Ethiopian Orthodox church would immediately begin stirring up trouble for the Ethiopian Christians.

Rick had just been in Ethiopia, sharing the gospel and training disciplemakers. The people had been responsive, and though the Orthodox priest in that area was very opposed to the Christians, Rick had experienced no difficulty with him while they were there. But the week of training was over now.

Before Rick and the other Americans left, Rick had prayed with the three disciplemakers who had worked with him. "Keep on in the Lord's work," he had said encouragingly. The three local believers had nodded and vowed to do so.

Then Rick and the team boarded a plane and flew back over the ocean to America. The disciplemakers were left in Ethiopia with many new believers who needed to be instructed, formed into churches, and taught to study the Bible—and with an angry Orthodox priest.

The priest had immense power over the area. He knew many influential people and he could get them to do many things for him. For the right price, these people would tell whatever lie he wanted.

One day, the disciplemakers were leaving a home where they had talked with the believers about growing their Bible study into a full house church. As they stepped out into the street, people began muttering and pointing. They glanced towards the disciplemakers with fierce glares on their faces. One even spat at the Christians' feet. The disciplemakers looked at each other anxiously. What had happened? Why were the people so angry?

The next day the three disciplemakers were summoned to court.

"They told lies about the Orthodox leaders!" the witness shouted, pointing at the Christians. "They are rabble-rousers, trouble-makers!"

The disciplemakers stood before the judge, frightened. The court was filled with angry people pressing in on every side, clearly in strong support of the witness's accusations. The disciplemakers were confused. They hadn't done anything! Why were these lies being told about them?

The witness sat down, only for another to leap up in his place. "Not only that!" the man said confidently. "They burned down the buildings on the far side of town."

The Christians' mouths dropped open. They stared around at the crowd, convinced that no one would believe this. But the response was only hostile faces. In panic, one of the disciplemakers opened his mouth to plead their innocence—but the gavel fell.

The judge sat up, looking down at the three Christians. "I have heard the accusations against you, and I find you guilty."

The disciplemakers felt a cold blow to their chests, as if someone had struck them. No... these were all lies, all completely false. They had done nothing! Sweat beaded on their foreheads. *How could they stop this?*

"You are each sentenced to seven years in prison." He slammed his gavel down, and the courtroom exploded into clamor. The three disciplemakers just stood there, in the middle of the shouting, seething court, staring numbly at the floor. Their hands were tingling as though they were just waking up from a deep sleep. *Seven years.* Seven years in prison.

During the ride to the prison there had been time for everything to sink in. It was a known fact that the Orthodox priest was a close friend of the judge who had sentenced them. There was no doubt where the false accusations had come from. That day, in that courtroom, in a matter of hours, everything had changed.

Now, sitting on a bare, cold cot, his hands clasped in front of him, one of the disciplemakers began to remember—what seemed like ages ago—how he and his friends had been so eager to plant churches and share the gospel and pray with other believers.

The disciplemaker got up from the bed and walked out of the room. His two friends were standing in the courtyard, gazing up at the huge walls surrounding them. He approached slowly and stopped a few feet away.

"Come," he said quietly. They turned to look at him, their faces lost and exhausted.

He tried to work up a smile. "Our families can visit us here, and I'm sure they will soon. For now, let's go and pray."

The two murmured a faint, "Yes," and cast another look at the high walls.

"Come," the disciplemaker said again. They turned and followed him into the prison compound.

Months passed.

Rick heard about what had happened: the priest's anger, the false witnesses, the court ruling and the disciplemakers being thrown in prison. He got the word out to believers all around the world to pray. Behind the scenes, he worked with advocacy organizations to try to get the men released. Then on his next trip to Ethiopia, Rick hurried to the prison to see the three Christians he had trained.

Rick was admitted through the gate and into the courtyard. There he waited while his friends were summoned. Rick looked around the courtyard; a gigantic rock-pile loomed a few feet away, where some men in inmates' clothes were breaking rocks apart with sledgehammers. Rick had had no word directly from the disciplemakers. He wondered how they were doing. Had they continued to trust God? Or had they become angry and bitter?

The guard returned, and behind him were the three disciplemakers. Rick waved to them. They saw him—and their faces broke into huge smiles. "Rick!" one shouted. They hurried to him and embraced, laughing and slapping him on the back.

Rick was a little shocked, but overjoyed. They seemed to be well, better than when he had left them. What had happened to make them so happy?

"Are you alright, then?" Rick asked, looking over each one in turn.

They sobered and turned towards each other, seeming to silently agree on something. Then one of them looked straight at Rick and said, "This has been the best experience of our lives."

The disciplemaker gestured to the compound. His voice was brimming with joy. "I never took studying the Bible seriously. I didn't spend time in prayer; I didn't understand the importance of telling others about God. But now, trapped in here, I read God's word daily and I pray to him constantly. He is revealing deeper and deeper truths to me every day. And we have been able to share our faith with many, many people."

"We can choose what room we stay in," another disciplemaker began. "At first we stayed together. But then we realized how many more people we could reach by splitting up. We each live in different sections of the compound now, so that we can tell the people near us about God."

"And every day," the third added, "We come together and lead a Bible study for the prisoners."

Rick shook his head in awe. The three disciplemakers stood facing him, smiling.

Rick was proud of them for standing strong. But he was even more amazed and encouraged by the outreach that they had begun here, in a prison—as prisoners, no less.

"I hear your case is on appeal," Rick said at last. Their time was coming to an end. "Maybe you will be cleared of your charges."

The disciplemakers firmly shook hands with Rick. "Maybe we will," one said. "If so, that will be God's will. But maybe it is His plan for us to remain here and continue to strengthen His kingdom in this place."

The others nodded. "If He asks us to stay here, even the rest of our lives," another said, "We will be willing to do so."

"God is doing great things," the third said with a grin.

Again Rick found himself staring at the three Ethiopian Christians, astounded by their faith. "Yes," he said softly. "He most certainly is."

Evangelism + Justice = Restoration

More than food, clean water, or medical assistance, people need Jesus. Still, over 3 billion people don't know him. That's why e3 Partners is on a strategic mission to launch one million new churches before the end of the decade. However, we can't just tell people about his love for them. We've got to show it.

Our expeditions offer opportunities to meet people at their greatest point of need. You can help prevent human trafficking, offer life-changing medical care, or alleviate the effects of poverty while introducing people to Jesus.

This is your church's chance to do something tangible about issues that truly matter.

e3partners.org/causes

Protection or Destruction?

A gathering of the forces of the Body of Christ had met on the Island of Cyprus—the same place where Paul, Timothy and Barnabas had ministered together. The Middle East leader of Frontiers was present, as was the Southern Baptist leader of Iraq. Many others had come as well, including Dan Hitzhusen from e3 Partners. They had gathered because of the war in Iraq. The Body of Christ believed that the time of turmoil and fear would present great opportunities to minister in Iraq, and for four days they planned together how to reach the Iraqi people for Christ.

When the meetings were over, Dan approached the Southern Baptist leader, who lived in Baghdad, Iraq.

"What do you really need the most?" Dan asked him.

The leader thought for a moment, and then said, "I need a prayer team to come to Baghdad and pray down the strongholds of the enemy. I need intercessors."

Dan had never led a short-term mission prayer team before. He didn't know what all it would entail. But he felt the Holy Spirit prompting him to say yes.

"I'll put together a team," Dan said. "We'll come to Baghdad and pray."

Dan returned to the United States and spent a good deal of time in prayer. This trip would be fraught with danger, and he didn't want to make any decisions without clear guidance from the Lord. He asked for a team to be raised up to go to Iraq.

Several people volunteered to be a part of the team, but before Dan accepted them he asked them if they knew for certain that God was calling them on this trip. Normally, when putting together a team, Dan told interested believers, "You don't need a call. God has already commanded you to 'Go' through the Great Commission. Really, you should say to God, 'Lord, I am going—unless you tell me not to.'" This time, however, the danger was so real and serious that Dan required the volunteers to not only spend time in prayer and Scripture, but to get the prayer and wisdom of the elders of their church and afterwards to be able to tell him that they were absolutely positive God wanted them to go on this trip. There would be a good chance of them not coming back.

Some of the volunteers withdrew, not being able to discern a direct call to the trip. Others Dan advised to withdraw, for the same reason. After two months elapsed, a team had been assembled of people who knew the risk and also knew that God had called them to be a part of this mission.

Most of the team members were from America, but another couple from Israel also planned to join them on the trip—Avi Mizrachi, the head of the Messianic Jewish congregations in Israel, and his wife Chaya, an American-born Messianic Jew. However, a short time before the team was set to leave, the elders of Avi's church told him that they had been praying about the trip, and they were certain that God had told them Chaya should go—but Avi should not. Avi was shaken. He should let his wife go alone into a war zone, where she might face death? Though his heart ached at the thought, nonetheless Avi consented to the wisdom of the elders and agreed to stay behind.

In order to get into Baghdad, the team would need to begin in Jordan and cross the Iraqi border at a checkpoint. Avi accompanied his wife on the journey to Jordan to meet up with the team from America. When Dan and the team arrived, Avi prayed over them all and anointed them with oil. The atmosphere was solemn. Would they give their lives in this mission?

As Avi poured the oil over his wife's head, his sober countenance shuddered and he broke into tears. Chaya wrapped her arms around him, and he buried his face in her hair. They hugged each other fiercely, both longing to be together during this dangerous journey—but both believing that God's will was different. They knew they had to trust Him.

The next day the team would begin their journey to the border. That night, Chaya had a vision. She saw two swords crossed over her head. There was nothing else. The image stayed with Chaya when she awoke, as if it was imprinted on her mind. Swords, poised just over her head. What could it mean? Were the swords a sign of protection? Or of impending doom?

In the twilight greyness of early morning, the team piled into four white SUVs. There was a big sign on each of the SUVs, showing a gun with a red slash through it and bold letters that declared, "No Guns On Board." The drivers of the caravan wanted to make it clear that the group was not military. And definitely, Dan's cover story for their trip was quite the opposite of a military mission.

The team was traveling as part of a fabricated tour group called "Taste and See Tours." It was a reference to the Bible verse, "Taste and see that the Lord is good" (Psalm 34:8a). But Dan's explanation was that their tour group really wanted to experience the culture of Iraq, wanted to get down deep and "taste and see."

After Dan made sure the entire team was loaded into the four vehicles, he hopped into one of the SUVs himself. The team members already seated inside watched as he shut the door and settled down into his seat.

The driver, a local Jordanian, turned around to look at them. "Alright," he said. "The deal is that one out of every four caravans is being hit by RPG rockets. We're going to drive as fast as we can, without stopping, to lower the risk. Are you all ready to go?"

They nodded, a few of them unconsciously gripping the sides of their seats. The driver turned back to the front and fired up the engine.

The Jordanian border was only an hour and a half away. The vehicles moved rapidly down the road, the drivers wary and silent. Within Jordan they were relatively safe, but once they got past the border checkpoint they would be in Iraqi territory. That is, if they could get past the border checkpoint.

Before long, the four SUVs approached the checkpoint. It was really more of a military outpost, with stern-faced men standing all around, holding machine guns in their arms. The caravan was stopped by the border officers, and the process of examination began. The vehicles had to be searched, and everyone's passport had to be checked inside the office.

Chaya, as an American now living in Israel, had two passports. She had used her Israeli passport to get into Jordan but had hoped to use her American passport to get into Iraq. Unfortunately, the rule was that you had to leave a country with the same passport by which you entered. Chaya had to present her Israeli passport to the officers.

They scanned the passport and then looked up at her. Chaya's hands were shaking uncontrollably. *Why didn't I use my other passport?* she thought desperately. Now she was entering Iraq as a Jew.

"Come with me," the officer said commandingly. Chaya froze. What was going to happen?

"Come," he said again, his eyes narrowed. Helpless and afraid, Chaya stumbled after him. As she was led away, she looked back at her teammates. They watched her, horrified, not knowing what to do. With a tremor Chaya faced forward, biting back a sob of fear, and followed the armed officials to the back of the building.

For Students In
Grades 6-8:
The Dog Walk

Designed to be done by the kids on their own!

Interrogation and the Secret Police

Dan walked up to the team waiting in the checkpoint office. He frowned. "Where's Chaya?" he asked.

The team members whirled around as he spoke, their faces betraying their distress. "Dan! They took Chaya back for questioning!"

Dan took in a sharp breath and looked towards the back of the office, which was guarded by armed soldiers. Somewhere in there Chaya was being questioned.

"Wait here and pray," Dan said in a low voice. The team nodded anxiously. Dan turned and began to walk up to the gate, not too slowly, not too quickly, keeping his expression neutral.

The rule is, he thought, *if you look like you own the place, you can go wherever you want.* He walked straight towards the guards, not even acknowledging them, and moved into the restricted area. The guards didn't stop him from proceeding. With his gaze fixed firmly ahead, Dan strode into the back of the office. After a few tense moments, he turned a corner and was out of sight.

Dan began walking down the halls looking for Chaya. He was worried—about her, and about the information she might disclose. The problem was that Dan had gone through interrogation training with all the other members of the team, who were from America, but not with Chaya. She had only joined the team when they arrived in Jordan. With the rest of the team, Dan had simulated an interrogation in which he yelled questions at them and they had to remain calm and cool. He had taught them what to answer and how to answer, and he had given them practice keeping their minds clear under pressure. He had also warned them about interrogators called "friendlies" who actually were the ones who got the most out of you. Rather than yelling and threatening you, they acted kind and nice and put you at your ease—when you would be more likely to let information slip.

But Chaya had had no such training. Dan peeked into one room after the other, nodding to the officials as he passed. Then he heard the sound of voices, and beneath them, a faint sobbing. Quickening his steps, Dan hurried down a side hall and reached an open doorway.

Chaya was sitting in a chair, her head bowed, crying desperately. In front of her stood three officers, who were asking her hard, pointed questions about the trip, the team, and their purpose in Iraq. Chaya was terrified, and in her panic she was saying far too much.

Dan walked swiftly into the room and went to Chaya's chair. He put his hand on her shoulder. "Just answer their questions," he said in a low, even tone. "No more, no less." He smiled encouragingly at her and then turned to the men conducting the questioning.

"Hi there, I'm Dan Hitzhusen," he said cheerfully. "I'm the leader of our group. Good to meet you."

The men were taken off guard by Dan's casual, lively interaction. They began chatting freely with him, and before long Dan had them laughing. The four men played around good-naturedly, joking and exchanging stories.

Then the leader stepped towards Dan and said quietly, so that no one else could hear, "My name is Abdul—but that is not what is on my name tag." Dan listened, surprised. What did the man mean?

"I am a member of the Jordanian secret police. I've been stationed at this checkpoint to keep an eye on things." He looked steadily at Dan and said, "If you have any trouble, let me know. You are free to go—you and your friend."

Dan looked at Abdul in amazement. This man had opened up to Dan, a complete stranger, and had promised them his help. *Well,* Dan thought heartily, *I'm not complaining about having a member of the Jordanian secret police on our side!*

Gently leading Chaya by the arm, Dan said goodbye to his new friends and walked out of the room. At the front of the building, the team welcomed Chaya and Dan with exclamations of relief. By now the SUVs had been searched, and the officials informed them that they could all go through. The team began to smile. It looked like they would actually get past the checkpoint without any major crisis.

"But we're going to have to keep your drivers here," the official said.

The team stared at him, and then at each other. What would they do without their drivers?

"One moment," Dan told the official. He turned and walked back past the armed soldiers and back into the restricted area to find Abdul.

Abdul looked up as Dan came down the hallway, amused to see him back so soon. "What is it?" he asked pleasantly.

Dan explained the situation, and Abdul nodded. "Oh yes, of course." He summoned a courier and said, "You! Tell the soldiers to let the entire caravan pass—along with their drivers."

"Yes sir!" the courier answered quickly and hurried off.

Grinning, Dan thanked Abdul for his help. The man smiled, nodding again. "Anytime."

Dan returned to his team, where the officials, slightly bewildered, told them and their drivers that they could all pass. Together the four SUVs moved through the gates and across the border of Jordan.

As his SUV drove past the exit, Dan looked out the window at the soldiers with their machine guns in their arms. He couldn't keep back a smile. *God works in strange ways sometimes.* If Chaya had not been interrogated, Dan wouldn't have met Abdul, and then they wouldn't have all gotten across the border—with their drivers. What seemed like a potential disaster was actually a means to their deliverance.

With a roar, their driver slammed his foot on the gas. Everyone inside the SUV was thrown back as the vehicle zoomed forward in a gush of churning dust. Behind and ahead of them, Dan could see the other SUVs racing forward at the same pace, leaving the outpost behind in a matter of seconds.

"What's going on?" one of the team members shouted, clutching the side of the car to keep from bouncing into his neighbor's seat.

"We're in Iraq now," the driver replied grimly, leaning over the steering wheel. "It's full speed ahead."

Painting Targets

At least, Dan thought, *the roads are straight.*

They had been bumping and rattling inside the SUV at 120 miles an hour for almost 10 hours. Grimly gripping the steering wheel, the driver kept the SUV speeding down the flat, straight Iraqi roads towards Baghdad.

Knowing that the trip would be a long one, Dan had brought two movies to watch on the way. The first was called *The Mission*. After the opening sequence, in which a missionary dies a shocking death, the team stared at the screen, looking slightly pale.

"Um...can we watch a different one?" a woman asked nervously.

Dan stuck in his second DVD—*Terminator 3*. While not exactly soothing, the fictional action movie distracted them from the rollicking ride and the worries of the travel. Then the Terminator said a line which set them all laughing: "Your levity is good. It reduces tension and fear of death."

"I think we need some levity," one of the men said, chuckling, "to reduce our fear of death!"

The rest of the team cracked up, and soon they were laughing so hard that several of them couldn't breathe. Throughout the trip, that line became their slogan: "Your levity is good. It reduces tension and fear of death!" Never, on any other trip, did Dan laugh more than during that trip to Baghdad.

After 12 hours of driving at 120 miles an hour, the caravan of vehicles made it safely to Baghdad. That night Dan and the others settled down in their hotel rooms to try to get some rest. It was difficult, however, to sleep peacefully when they could hear tanks rolling down the street outside and constant machine gun fire peppering the air and bombs exploding in different parts of the city. Baghdad was in a chaotic time.

When Dan awoke the next morning, still sleepy from his fitful rest, he gathered the team together for prayer. The Southern Baptist leader had arranged a place for them to meet and pray—the house of an Iraqi general, in the ambassador district. The team went to this house every morning and spent an hour praying individually, kneeling on cushions that the leader had provided. After this time, they spent an hour praying in small groups. Then they talked together about what the Holy Spirit had spoken to them in prayer.

Many times, all the groups had received the same word. They assembled the prayer requests that God had led them to pray that day, and then sent them out in an email to 70,000 people who were waiting to pray for what the team had listed. The team felt that they were Special Forces on a mission to "paint targets" for the "troops." They had come in and were doing local research to find out what God wanted to be prayed for in the high risk situation. Then they were contacting the "air troops" to come in and "bomb" those targets with the 70,000 prayer warriors. It was an exciting time.

After the morning spent in prayer, the team met with a group of Iraqi Christians and trained them how to share their faith using the EvangeCube, so that they could witness boldly during the war. Then the team visited the University of Baghdad and prayer-walked the campus. They had the opportunity to share the gospel with a number of Iraqi students.

As the team traveled through Baghdad, they stopped by a parade ground where Saddam

Hussein used to march his troops. There was a large monument that the troops would march under which was formed by two gigantic swords. Chaya saw it and remembered the vision she had had. Was this the image from her dream? Was this the two crossed swords? She didn't know for sure. As the team walked back to their hotel, Chaya was quieter than usual, reflecting on what she had seen.

With them on this trip was Tom Doyle, e3 Partners' Middle East Director. Tom knew Paul Bremmer, the US ambassador to Iraq, who was living in the palace at Baghdad. As an ambassador in a warzone, Paul Bremmer was extremely influential and had a lot of power. He was even called "King Paul." Tom had been able to arrange a meeting with Paul Bremmer to spend some time praying for him.

The day of the meeting arrived, and the team went to Saddam Hussein's former palace to await their appointment. Paul Bremmer sent one of his aides to escort the team through the gates into what was called the "green zone." This was where all the United States military was stationed. It was strange to walk into such a tight, organized camp, filled with American soldiers, after spending time in the city. Everywhere they looked there were military personnel and huge army tanks. There was a war going on, and the high security gave the team an even deeper awareness of the fact.

The aide led the team into the palace, where Paul Bremmer stepped out of a meeting with the Iraqi cabinet to see them. After exchanging greetings, Paul bowed his head and the team huddled around him. They prayed for his work, his position, and the great burden which he was bearing. They asked God to lead him and give him wisdom. For about half an hour the team prayed, while the Iraqi cabinet in the next room waited patiently for Paul's return.

When the team finished praying, the ambassador shook their hands and thanked them for coming to pray for him. Then he resumed his meeting, and his aide led the team on a tour of Saddam Hussein's palace, including the 12,000 square foot throne room. Afterwards, the aide escorted them back to the entrance. The team walked past the US tanks and soldiers, out through the front gates, and into the streets of Baghdad, where the gun fire still rattled in the distance.

The Two Swords

The market-place hummed with activity. Brightly colored awnings shaded wares of every kind, from jewelry and antiques to cloth and spices. Dan meandered through the alleys, delightedly taking in the beautiful, brilliant products, all resplendent with Arabian culture. Around him crowds of people were passing by, stopping to purchase from the vendors or to look over the items that were displayed.

The team had taken a day off to wander the city and do a little shopping. Soon they would be heading back to Jordan, and each team member wanted to take something from the city back with them. Dan ducked beneath the shade of an awning. The man there had a varied display of antique items, and foremost among them was a pair of gorgeous, ancient swords. Dan stared at them in admiration. He had a large collection of swords and knives and weapons from the places he had visited, but these swords were the most beautiful ones he had ever seen.

"How much are the swords?" Dan asked the man. Soon Dan was walking back through the marketplace with the swords carefully wrapped and tucked under his arm, a contented smile on his face.

The night before they were to leave, the team packed up the SUVs, and early the next morning the four SUVs pulled out of Baghdad and headed back to the border. The team watched the buildings of the city slide past the windows and thought back on all that had happened. Their mission had been accomplished. They had spent precious time in prayer throughout Baghdad, and God had come through in amazing ways.

Dan could see that Chaya had grown during the trip. She was a pastor's wife, used to working in the background. But now her kids had grown up and left the house, and she had come on this trip, a dangerous mission into a war zone, without her husband. Though she missed Avi, Chaya had been able to delve into aspects of herself that she hadn't before. She had grown bolder. She had stepped into a new position of ministry, and Dan felt that God would be using that in great ways in the coming years.

The SUVs drove out of the city and onto the long, flat roads across Iraq. Once again the drivers stepped on the gas, sending the speedometer leaping up to 120 miles an hour. The SUVs veritably flew across the land, rushing and jolting back to the border like a flock of scattered birds. In the back of the vehicles the team sat together, talking quietly amongst themselves and continuing to laugh together as they had throughout the journey.

After 10 hours of driving, the SUVs arrived back at the border again. Everyone climbed out of the vehicles to allow the officials to search the SUVs. Again, all passports were checked, and again, Chaya had to present her Israeli passport.

"Where's Chaya?" Dan asked a short while later.

"She got taken in for questioning again," the team member told him, glancing worriedly down the hall.

Chaya, as a Jew in Iraq, had immediately triggered the officials' suspicion and wariness. Now she was having to undergo interrogation again, after already being taken in on the way to Baghdad. Dan knew that she would be scared.

For the second time this trip, Dan walked past the armed guards and back into the office. He found the room where Chaya was being held. She was sitting in a chair, as before, while the men were questioning her. Dan came in and quietly sat down by her side. Chaya's shoulders slumped in relief, and she smiled gratefully at him.

The men doing the questioning were unfamiliar. Dan didn't see Abdul anywhere, so he simply stayed with Chaya and helped her answer the questions calmly and safely. Everything seemed to be going smoothly, and Dan prayed that they would be able to pass the checkpoint without trouble.

Then a man walked into the room, carrying two long, ancient swords. Dan winced slightly and dropped his head. *Oh, no...* he thought.

"These are antiques," said the man with a frown. "You can't bring them back with you."

Dan bit his lip. "I was hoping to add them to a collection of mine," he said hopefully. "They're beautiful swords."

The man's face remained stern. One of the officials, however, walked over and picked up one of the swords. He inspected it curiously. Then his boyish nature got a hold of him. With a flourish he pulled the sword from its sheath and brandished it, starting to grin. It really was a fantastic weapon.

Dan picked up the other sword, and pulled it from its sheath as well. He playfully got into a fighting stance, and, chuckling, the other man matched his posture. With much laughter and slow-motion cuts and parries, they started to mock-swordfight around the room. Chaya sat in her chair, watching them. Then Dan and the man crossed their swords once more—right over her head.

The image sprang out at her, startlingly clear. In that moment she saw her vision. This was the picture God had shown her before the trip began; this was the time the dream had been speaking of. And suddenly she knew what God had been telling her through the dream. For the span of this trip, God had made Dan her protector.

As Dan held the ancient sword in his hand, blocking the other man's weapon over her head, Chaya thanked God for revealing His message to her.

After the swordplay, the men were friendly and open towards Dan and Chaya. The officials allowed them both to leave the room and go back to the SUVs. Once all the vehicles were checked and all the papers and passports were confirmed, the caravan was waved through the checkpoint and back into Jordan. Within two hours the team had arrived at the house from where they had started. Avi greeted them ecstatically, embracing his wife and praising God for bringing them all back safely.

Before the Americans went home, Dan anointed Chaya with oil. He firmly believed that God had opened up the next stage in her life. In a step of faith, she had accepted His call to go on this trip and had trusted Him to lead her. During the journey she had experienced His power and guidance. Now Dan felt that there was a new place for her in ministry. Together the team dedicated Chaya for this service in which God would use her.

The team flew home and returned to their families back in America. The time they had spent in Iraq stayed with them, reminding them to pray for the national believers who were continuing to risk their lives to share the gospel with the Iraqi people. They also prayed for the frightened people who were living in the war zone without knowledge of Jesus, unable to see any hope. This had been Dan's first time leading a prayer team, and he thanked God for guiding what they did and giving them the requests for which to pray.

There was only one thing that bothered him about the trip. Despite their favorable attitudes towards Dan and Chaya, the officials at the checkpoint had refused to let Dan keep the pair of swords. They had confiscated them and Dan had had to leave behind those two gorgeous, ancient swords somewhere in Jordan. Dan sighed mournfully, contemplating the memory. They were the nicest swords that he had ever owned.

Restoration

It's an inescapable theme in the Bible. In the midst of our greatest darkness, Jesus stepped out of heaven to restore peace, justice, and bring salvation through his work on the cross and his victory over death.

As his followers, we're called to join his campaign and take the Gospel to the darkest corners of this world. We seek restoration for the oppressed, the marginalized, and the overlooked. But doing this effectively is easier said than done.

That's why the right partnership makes all the difference.

www.e3partners.org

Let's Pray Again

    The missionary team had split up between five different Nepali villages, dividing into groups of two Americans, translators, and a member of the local church. By separating, the missionaries would be able to speak the gospel to a greater number of people.
    Jim and his teammate had been assigned to a rice farming village. Here in the rice farming community, the homes were small, poor dwellings, constructed of mud and thatch. Jim and his team moved through the village, visiting the different neighborhoods and stopping to chat with the families. The team shared the gospel with all those they met, and even when the villagers were not responsive to the message, they were still open and friendly. Jim and the others were able to share good, heartfelt conversations with them.
    In one house they entered, a woman was visiting her friends there. She listened to Jim tell about God and His almighty power. When Jim finished speaking, she said hesitantly, "My husband has been paralyzed for six months. Would you come to my home and pray for him?"
    The woman was a Hindu. Jim heard the desperation in her voice and realized that she wasn't so much seeking after God—she was looking for any way, any miracle, that might help her husband.
    "I would be glad to come pray for him," Jim said kindly.

The woman led Jim and his team to her house. Inside, the light was low, and the walls of the hut seemed murky with shadows. Jim narrowed his eyes to see more clearly. In the corner of the hut a man lay silently on a hard reed mat. As Jim walked through the doorway the man turned his head, every move heavy with lethargy. His eyes were dull, his beard grown long and straggly, and his skin coated with dirt and grime. His entire left side was pinned to the ground, lifeless.

Jim felt a surge of compassion for him, knowing how terrible it must be to live in this weakened state. The man was unable to work in the fields to support his wife and was dependent on her help just to stand up.

The woman went to her husband's side, speaking softly to him. Jim followed her. "May I pray for you?" Jim asked. He knelt down beside the mat.

The man looked at his wife, and she took his hand in hers. "Yes," the man said to Jim. "Please."

Jim lifted his hands and laid them on the man's left shoulder. Cold sweat turned his skin clammy, and Jim took a steadying breath.

Praying over people was still not something Jim was completely comfortable doing. He had grown up in a church where certain spiritual gifts were said to have ceased. After traveling with e3 Partners and witnessing miracles all around the world, Jim knew that God did indeed still work through healing. But this skepticism was so engrained into Jim's character, that every time he prayed he had to ask God to increase his faith.

So before Jim prayed out loud for this paralyzed man, he said a prayer for his own heart. "Lord," Jim prayed silently. "I know you can heal this man if you choose. Please—don't let my unbelief get in the way of Your power."

Jim met the man's eyes. "Remember, it is my God who has the ability to heal—not me. I am going to pray that He will demonstrate his power in you." Jim closed his eyes, and began to pray.

For five minutes Jim entreated God's power over the man's paralyzed arm. He spoke boldly, knowing that God would answer if it was His will. At last Jim opened his eyes. "Amen," he said.

The man looked at Jim, as if wondering what to do next. Jim gestured to his arm. "Has there been any change?"

The man lowered his gaze to his stiff arm. His brow furrowed in concentration, and then... he lifted his arm away from his side. He gasped. At about six inches from his side, the man stopped. He couldn't lift his arm any further. But he was already overwhelmed. He hadn't been able to move his arm a fraction for six months.

Jim felt the Holy Spirit stirring inside him. "Let's pray again," he said. The man glanced at him in surprise. Jim laid his hands on the shoulder again and began to pray.

"Amen," Jim finished. He nodded to the man. "Try your arm now."

The man raised his arm six inches from his side—then nine inches...then a foot. He stared at his own limb as if it was a foreign object. Tentatively, he moved his arm back and forth. The shoulder was rotating again.

"Well, let's pray again," Jim said. Once more, Jim touched the man's shoulder and asked God to restore its mobility. "Amen."

The man looked from Jim to his arm, and then, without being prompted, he tried to lift it again. He could raise it all the way above his head. His wife covered her mouth with her hands, her eyes teary. The man moved his arm behind him, in front of him, over his head, then back down to his side. He was almost laughing with joy.

Jim smiled. Then he looked down at the man. His left leg was still stuck straight out in front of him. Jim felt that God had not yet revealed His greatest glory.

"Your arm is working now?" Jim said. The man grinned, clenching his left fist. "Then now let's pray over your leg."

Jim placed his hands on the man's petrified limb. And again, through the power of the Holy Spirit, Jim asked God to glorify His name in the man's body. By the end of the prayer, the man could move his leg a little.

They prayed again. The man could bend his knee and draw his leg up to his chest. They prayed again. Then Jim and the man's wife helped him stand up on his feet. The man was shaky; he hadn't used his left leg for six months. Holding onto his cane for support, the man stepped from the house and out into his front yard. He blinked in the sunlight, his hands trembling on his cane.

He turned towards Jim. "Thank you," he breathed. Tears streamed freely down his dirt-stained face, disappearing into his beard. "You have healed me! Thank you, thank you—" he fell to his knees, sobbing, and grabbed onto Jim's ankles.

Jim quickly got down on his knees and broke the man's hold. "No," he said firmly. "It was not I who healed you. Only God, the one true God, has the power to heal. I am His servant. I am here to show you His might and strength."

The man looked at Jim in wonder. "Can you tell me about Him?" he asked.

Jim talked with both the man and his wife that day, and the next day he returned to their house. The man greeted Jim at the door, smiling. He had washed himself, and he was newly shaven and dressed in fresh clothes. There was no sign of the cane.

Jim spent many hours talking with the man. He told him the gospel and how Jesus had healed many people on earth. The man listened hungrily. He loved hearing the stories from Jim, for he couldn't read and so couldn't learn them for himself. Over the next five days, Jim came to the man's house every day and told him Bible stories. Every day the man eagerly welcomed Jim into his house with a warm smile. And every day the man's limbs grew stronger. By the end of five days, the man was ready to return to work. His body was completely normal.

On that last day the man took Jim outside into his yard. "You see that temple?" the man said, pointing to a small structure behind his house. "I worshipped many Hindu idols there. But now—I am going to destroy it." His face was solemn, and his eyes, as Jim watched, burned with passion.

"There is only one true God, and that is Jesus Christ," the man said. "I am going to get rid of the idols and this temple. It is Jesus and He alone that I will worship."

For Students In Grades 8-12:
Cat and Dog Theology

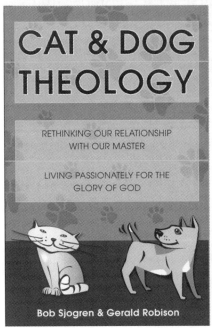
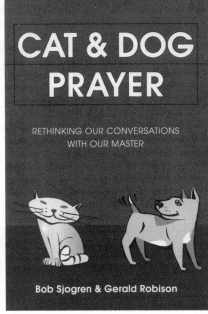

Chicago?

Lord, give me the words to say, Jennifer prayed. *I have no idea what I'm doing, but I'll trust you to accomplish Your work through me.*

Jennifer was walking down a hot, dusty road in the rural countryside of India. Her only companions were an interpreter, an intercessor, and a village local, all of whom were strangers to her. She was the only American. The rest of her team was an hour or more away, back in town or off on ministry outreaches of their own. She felt very alone.

The little team was traveling to a Meitei village to share the gospel. The Meteis were Hindus who worshipped snakes. They had an ancient book which told them about the snake who won the battle in the Garden of Eden. Jennifer was there to tell them the rest of the story. The thought caused a fresh wave of nervousness to shiver through her. *Please, Lord,* she prayed again, as the small village huts came into view. *Use me.*

The Meitei people lived simply, without electricity or running water, with no televisions or phones. They had no connection to global news and though they knew their own area well, they were completely unaware of the world as a whole. It was a huge event to have an American visit their village.

When the village local took Jennifer to a house, the people instantly began to gather. Over a hundred villagers came to hear Jennifer speak, if just out of curiosity. The faces of the people were bright, inquisitive, and smiling. Jennifer got up in front of them, her hands clammy and shaking.

"Hello," she said. "My name is Jennifer, and I have come to talk to you about my God."

Jennifer went on to share her testimony, and as she spoke the words came easier, her voice stopped trembling, and her heartbeat settled back into a steady rhythm. She felt God guiding her presentation. "I serve the one true God, my King, and I have come because God loves the Meiteis, and He wants you to know about Him," she said.

She began the full story of the gospel, describing man's sin and how God loved them so much that He sent His own Son to take their penalty, that Jesus had risen again, and that the salvation He purchased was a free gift to all people.

Right in the middle of her sentence, a man in the back of the room suddenly raised his hand. Jennifer paused. Awkwardly, she turned to her interpreter. He walked over to the man, everyone's eyes following him.

As the two men talked, a single word reached Jennifer's ear, a word she understood within the foreign language, one that sounded unbelievably strange and alien in this rural Indian village: Chicago.

Jennifer waited for her interpreter, confused and completely thrown off. Why would she hear the name of an American city here? These people had no way to connect with the outside world. They were isolated in the countryside of India—how did they even know the word Chicago?

The interpreter turned to Jennifer, shrugging. "He wants to know if you're from Chicago." The village man watched Jennifer excitedly, his eyes sparkling.

"Well, yes," Jennifer answered hesitantly. "I live in San Diego now, but I guess I really am from Chicago—that's where I was born and raised."

Her interpreter gave the message to the man. As soon as he had heard, the man smiled widely; he immediately turned and began talking with his neighbors. The interpreter nodded to Jennifer, letting her know that she could continue.

Unsettled by the weird incident, Jennifer scrambled to regain her train of thought. "If you accept Jesus as Your Lord and Savior, He will cleanse you from all sin and give you a new life in Him. You can know that when you die, you will spend forever in heaven with God," Jennifer finished. She took a deep breath, ready to offer the Meiteis an opportunity to pray for salvation.

But something halted her—a nagging sense in the back of her head, something that was out of place. She couldn't shake the queer feeling that the man and his question had given her.

Finally she looked out into the crowd and found where the older man was sitting. "Why did you ask if I was from Chicago?" she said. The interpreter translated the question.

The man got to his feet and began explaining rapidly, his hands gesturing in the air. Her interpreter listened until the man fell silent. Then he turned back to Jennifer, looking slightly shaken.

"He says," the interpreter began, "That they had a prophecy in this village—that someone from Chicago was going to come and tell them about the one true God." Jennifer felt her stomach twist peculiarly. "They just wanted to make sure they were listening to the right person," the interpreter said, beginning to grin.

Jennifer stared at the villagers, unable to keep her mouth from hanging ajar. They all looked up at her with huge smiles on their faces. Their prophecy had come true. Jennifer was here, as God had promised, and now they knew who this one true God was and how they could know Him personally.

When Jennifer managed to give the invitation, almost the entire assembly prayed to receive Jesus. The village was dramatically impacted by the fulfillment of God's word to them, and the number of new believers was staggering. Soon after, a new church was planted in this Meitei village.

Jennifer went back to the town and her team that night, struck deep with awe. God had given her the blessing of being involved in a work far greater than any she could have ever imagined.

The Book of Acts in Action

Four years before a team from e3 Partners had gone to India on a short-term mission trip. They had traveled to a state in India that had a population of 114 million people—and less than one percent of them were Christians. The team had partnered with a local pastor named G— (name withheld for security purposes) and, during the time that they were in India, they had worked in 17 villages and planted 42 house churches. The team had returned to America, and G—'s ministry had continued such that after two years had gone by, those 42 churches had multiplied into 710 churches.

Six months later, Dan was in Uganda giving training to key African nationals. While he was there, he received a report from India: in G—'s state of India, there were now 2602 churches. In February of the next year, Dan traveled to India again. There he witnessed the extraordinary fact that there were 5200 churches which had been planted as a result of those first 42.

Now, just a few months later, a total of over 8000 churches had been started. G—'s ministry was working in 1012 different areas of their state. In 15 of those areas, churches had been planted to the ninth, tenth, and eleventh generations, as each new church went on to plant a daughter church.

E3 Partners had taught this strategy of multiplication to all the churches they worked with. It was a simple, logical method, but it saw tremendous growth and expansion in the churches. Discipleship also was an invaluable tool. It allowed the new believers to be instructed and strengthened and gave them a heart to reach others. G—'s ministry was a wonderful example of these methods in practice. They were doing astonishing work in India.

This was the setting when, one day, Dan received an email from e3 Partners' president, Curtis Hail. Curtis Hail had a request from one of e3's donors for a report on discipleship.

"I wanted to ask you about discipleship," the donor had written. "What is an experience you've had with leading someone to Christ and then discipling them? What happened from there?"

Dan thought about it. He could think of several instances—but he knew someone who had even more stories than he did concerning discipleship. "Let me see what Pastor G— has to say about this," Dan murmured, pulling out his phone.

He texted G—, and within ten minutes the Indian pastor had replied. The message was several pages in length.

"Something instantly comes to my mind," G— wrote. Dan smiled. He had thought that might happen. What Dan read next was an incredible story of what can happen in a chain reaction of evangelism and discipleship.

Pastor G— had the opportunity to share the gospel with a man named Vikas, who was jobless and looking for work. Vikas accepted Christ as his Savior, and Pastor G— began to disciple him. Soon Vikas joined them in the ministry. A short while later, Vikas led some of them to a village where people needed prayer for healing. While Vikas was in the village, he shared the gospel with a young man selling alcohol. The man's name was Bajarang. Bajarang accepted Christ, and his life was dramatically changed. He became a witness to the entire village who had known what he was like before. Then Bajarang shared the gospel with a man named Kiran. Kiran used to make fun of the Christians constantly and ridicule their beliefs. When Barong witnessed to him, Kiran was convicted and stopped taunting the Christians, and he too accepted Christ as his Savior.

Kiran journeyed to another village. There he led a girl named Kavita to Christ. Dan grinned fondly as he read Pastor G—'s broken English: "Kavita was accepted Christ and began to read Bible." Kiran then discipled her. But Kavita was the only person in her entire village who believed in Jesus. It was a hard life for a little while. Before long, however, Kavita and Kiran had reached others for Christ and had started seven new churches in the village.

From there, Kavita went to a remote village. She met a young man named Sandeep and shared the gospel with him. He was saved and began attending a Christian small group. Now Sandeep is a leader of several small groups himself. Sandeep also shared the gospel with Raju.

Raju was suffering from depression because his wife had left him. But when Sandeep witnessed to him, Raju was saved and God began working in his life. Sandeep discipled Raju, and soon Raju had the opportunity to lead an elderly woman named Harnabai to Christ. Harnabai was a peddler; she would travel to remote villages and sell brooms door-to-door. After she accepted Christ, she continued to make her rounds, but now she told the gospel house-to-house before selling her brooms. Harnabai also started a church in her own house and discipled a young woman named Suvarna.

Suvarna had a heart disease, but God showed His glory and healed her. Then Suvarna met a lady named Jyothi, who had an awful relationship with her husband. They were always fighting. Suvarna shared her faith, and Jyothi asked Jesus to be her Lord and Savior.

"Now," G— concluded, "God has transformed Jyothi's life, and she is witnessing to many."

Dan shook his head in amazement. Just by one person leading one person to Christ and making the commitment to disciple them, huge numbers had been reached—and were continuing to be reached. Even as Dan read Pastor G—'s message, more churches were being planted and more people were being trained to share the gospel.

Many people thought that large-scale church multiplication was impossible. But Pastor G—'s story was an amazing example of the power of discipleship and the simple, achievable ways in which churches can multiply. A ministry that had begun four years before had started over 10,000 churches in that short period of time. This movement was what e3 Partners wanted to see all over the world— not churches lying stagnant, but churches multiplying and planting generations all around them because of the passion and faith of the believers.

Dan felt as if he were reading the Book of Acts as he read Pastor G—'s text. He thought about everything God had done through Paul and his missionary journey, and what God was doing now through Pastor G—and his key leaders. Dan scrolled through the message again, tears welling in his eyes. Pastor G—'s story was one of true obedience. He and his leaders were living out Jesus' final command on this earth: "Therefore go and make disciples of all the nations, baptizing them in the Name of the Father and of the Son and of the Holy Spirit, and teaching them to obey everything I have commanded you. And surely I am with you always, to the very end of the age" (Matthew 28:19-20).

Beyond Languages

Ten years ago, Dan and a team sent by e3 Partners had gone into Manipur, India, for the first time. They were the first foreigners to enter Manipur in 50 years. When they had arrived, the Naga tribe had welcomed them with a huge celebration. One hundred years before, an American named William Pettigrew had come and shared the gospel with the Nagas. Then, 100 years later, the Naga tribe had celebrated the team from America who had come to show them how to take the gospel to other peoples.

One of those people groups was the snake-worshiping Hindu tribe, the Meiteis. At the time of e3 Partners' first visit to Manipur, there were only 25 known churches among the Meitei and just a few hundred believers. Over the course of 10 years, e3 Partners sent about 68 short-term mission teams to Manipur to work with the Nagas in reaching the Meiteis for Christ.

Now, after 10 years, the number of churches had grown from 25 known churches to 1200 known churches. From a few hundred believers, now several thousand Meiteis were serving Christ. The Meiteis sent word to e3 Partners and told them, "We are now a reached people group. We are ready to take the gospel out to other tribes."

The Meiteis invited a team to come to Manipur for a huge celebration that would praise

God for the work that had been done amongst them. In answer to the request, Dan Hitzhusen and a select group of men and women flew into Manipur, India, and made their way to the Meitei tribe.

When they arrived, the team held trainings for their Meitei brothers and sisters and taught them how to share the gospel. Then the believers traveled to several villages where there weren't any churches yet, reaching out to the lost and proclaiming the message of Jesus Christ. During one of the trainings, a young Meitei girl performed a special worship dance. Dressed in traditional Meitei garb, she moved her arms through the air in twisting patterns, bouncing on her toes to the rhythm of their local music.

One of the women on Dan's team, Vicki was a dancer as well. She watched the Meitei girl dance, fascinated by this new form of worshipful movement.

Wouldn't it be awesome, Dan thought to himself, observing the two, *if this young girl and Vicki could dance together?*

He proposed the idea to the nationals. "What if, at the celebration service, Vicki and this talented young dancer perform a duet?"

The nationals looked at each other excitedly.

"That's a great idea," they said, grinning.

Soon the tribe was in a jubilant flurry of activity as they prepared for the celebration. People were scurrying this way and that, laughing and talking excitedly, and busily going about their tasks. Off to the side, the young girl was practicing a lively dance.

Dan was standing nearby. He saw Vicki go over and greet the young Meitei dancer. The two didn't have an interpreter, but soon they were moving to the music in their own unique styles, both young women smiling in delight. After a while the two of them withdrew, giggling, and carted off the music player with the impish furtiveness of children trying not to be caught.

This is really going to be neat, Dan thought fondly.

The evening of the service arrived, and word had gotten around that the young Meitei dancer and Vicki, the American woman, were going to be doing a dance together. All the Meiteis and the whole American team were thrilled to see what the two ladies had put together—and in such a short time!

The service began with the huge crowd of believers singing praise songs to the Lord. The worship was rousing and glorious—it seemed as if the room would burst with the joy of the Meiteis as they shouted glory to God for all the mighty things He had done. Then several people shared testimonies and stories from the ten years of ministry and outreach among the Meiteis. After each testimony, the crowd clapped and cheered, giving God more glory as they remembered the specific times when they had seen His power and love. Then more praise was sung, and all the voices of all the people gathered lifted into one harmonious roar of adoration. It was a time of pure celebration.

When the last song had died down and the people were still clapping and cheering, the two dancers came out. They set up their music player, and, exchanging small nervous smiles, got into position. The crowd fell silent, eagerly watching the Meitei girl and Vicki, the American, as the music began to play.

The Meitei girl stepped forward, pushing her hands down to her sides and then curving them up over her head. She danced to the beat, her feet lightly tapping out the accents in the music. Vicki, in contrast, danced expressively to the Meitei lyrics. Her hands and her body moved gracefully with gestures which interpreted the words into motion. The two dances were completely different, but they were each beautiful and stirring in their own way.

The Meiteis watched the dancers in amazement. They were astounded that the American woman could have learned the words to the song so quickly, and then have created motions that represented them so wonderfully.

When the song started to reach its climax, both dancers suddenly came together. They moved as one, creating a curious, gorgeous blend of both their dances in something completely new. With one final gesture the dancers finished their piece, and the entire assembly rose to their feet and began clapping furiously and shouting joyfully. Both Vicki and the Meitei girl were glowing with happiness. They glanced towards each other and laughed breathlessly.

After the service was over, many people came up and thanked the two dancers for sharing with them. The Meiteis expressed their amazement at how Vicki had learned the lyrics in the short period of time. When she heard their exclamations, she began to grin.

"I never learned the words," she said.

Everyone stared at her in shock. "But," one person said, confused, "Your moves went with the lyrics perfectly."

Vicki shook her head helplessly, her smile growing even wider.

Somehow, the Holy Spirit had moved in her dance and had guided her motions so that they beautifully and exactly matched the meaning of the Meitei song. Even at a celebration service, even in a worship dance, God's Spirit had directed and led, just as He had throughout the 10 years of work in Manipur. And as the Meiteis celebrated and prepared to reach out to others, God showed them His power yet again by allowing them to see the unity of the Body of Christ right there in their service—across continents, between cultures, and even beyond languages.

You Recruit the Team. We Get Them Ready.

Logistics. Airfare, lodging, translators, and meals — there are so many things to juggle and we manage it all. We basically do everything but pack for you!

Training. Is your team feeling unqualified? Welcome to the club! Everyone says that. We train your team on everything from sharing the Gospel to interacting with new cultures.

Fundraising. With our built-in crowd-funding platform and a wealth of available resources, you'll leave fully funded and make it look easy too.

e3partners.org/missions

Tell Them Why We're Here

Michelle was terrified. She looked out the dusty window of the van, out at the strange country passing by. She was in Ethiopia, miles away from her home, on her first mission trip with e3 Partners. Her team leader, Dan Hitzhusen, was up in the front of the bus, smiling cheerily.

Michelle looked down at her hands, nervously lacing her fingers together. It had been a huge test of her courage just to decide to go on this trip. Now they would be going out into Muslim and Orthodox villages, attempting to share the gospel.

At least Carl would be with her. Michelle was barely five feet tall and weighed less than 100 pounds. But Carl, her husband, was 6 foot 5 and 280 pounds and a Marine. Glancing over at him, Michelle felt her tension in her stomach relax. She felt safe with Carl. He would protect her.

The bus slowed, bumping over a few potholes, and braked to a halt. Michelle's interpreter, Metsfin, stood up. "This is our stop," he said to Michelle, in his thickly accented voice. He smiled kindly at her. Another wave of anxiety rushed over Michelle as she shakily stood up and moved down the aisle of the bus. She looked back at Carl, expecting to see him following behind her. But he was still in his seat, watching her anxiously.

"Wait," she said numbly, as Metsfin led her off the bus. "Is Carl...is he not coming?"

They stepped back as the bus roared to life and drove off down the road, sending up a spiraling cloud of dust. It drove off with Carl still inside.

Michelle watched the bus go, stunned into horrified silence. She was all alone with a few Ethiopian men whom she had only met a few days ago. Carl wasn't with her, and she wouldn't see him again until the end of the day. And she was now supposed to go share her faith in a Muslim and Orthodox Ethiopian village!

She slowly turned to Metsfin, who nodded encouragingly. "Come on," he said. "Let's walk down to the village."

One step at a time, Michelle reminded herself as their small group began moving away from the road towards the houses below.

As they reached the edge of the village, Michelle felt eyes beginning to follow them. The villagers watched them curiously from their yards and doorways, looking up from their work to see these unfamiliar visitors. They were especially fascinated by Michelle—a foreigner. She tried to avoid their eyes, hunching down even smaller than she was.

One of the villagers, a Muslim woman named Rebecca, came out to greet them. "Why have you come?" she asked pleasantly.

Metsfin turned to Michelle. She hesitated, and then said, "We've come to share about Jesus."

"I would like to hear," Rebecca said interestedly. "Please, come into my house and tell me."

Michelle stared wonderingly at Rebecca. Is it going to be this easy? Are people this eager to hear about the gospel?

They went inside the house and spoke to Rebecca for some time. Michelle shared her testimony, and afterwards she used the EvangeCube to present the gospel. The woman listened attentively to everything they said. Then she invited a bunch of her friends over to hear what the team had to say. Michelle spoke to all of them.

"Tomorrow, let's meet back here again as a group," she said.

They visited over thirty more homes, and shared their faith with the villagers there. After each meeting, Michelle asked the people if they would gather together with the other groups the next day. As it came time to leave, Michelle whispered to Metsfin, "Our group is going to be massive!" People had responded enthusiastically to the gospel, and they wanted to know more. There had been no ill will, no threats, and no glares. Michelle was starting to enjoy herself. She liked getting to meet new people and having the privilege of sharing her Lord with them.

"It's probably time to head back to where we were dropped off," Metsfin said at last.

"More like where we were *dumped in*," Michelle mumbled, still feeling a bit victimized from the shock she had been given that morning.

They gathered up their things, said goodbye to a few more villagers, and started the short trek to where the bus would pick them up. Arriving at the side of the road, they looked to the left and the right. The bus wasn't in sight yet. Just as Michelle was settling down to wait, a group of young Muslim and Orthodox men came striding up to the team. Their faces were angry and creased with frowns. Michelle shrank back fearfully as the group of about 50 men surrounded them.

"What are you doing here?" one of them asked aggressively.

Michelle swallowed hard. "W-what do I do?" she asked Metsfin, stammering.

"Just go ahead," he said quietly. "Just tell them why we're here."

Michele drew herself up, aware that her limbs were shaking visibly. "We're here to share with you—."

"We don't want to hear what you have to say," a man shouted, interrupting her. "You don't speak the truth!"

Michelle turned back to Metsfin, her terror mounting with every second. Metsfin looked around at the tense, aggravated crowd, and then he calmly said, "Let's start with the HOPE cube. Then we can at least get them listening."

He pulled the HOPE cube out of the pack and passed it to Michelle. The men watched her, talking amongst themselves in loud murmurs, their gazes threatening. Michelle stood up, taking a deep breath. Her heart was pounding like a hammer against her chest and her skin was cold with sweat. She had never been more scared in her life.

"There are many ways to prevent HIV/AIDs," Michelle said loudly. She held up the cube over the crowd. "These are a few practical ways to stay healthy and to stop the spread of the disease."

The men fell quiet, suddenly absorbed. This wasn't what they were expecting. They wanted to hear this message. They wanted to know what Michelle had to say about the deadly disease that had killed so many in their land.

Michelle turned through each panel of the HOPE cube, keeping her voice raised in order for everyone to hear. When she closed the cube, the men began talking again, excitedly.

"Keep talking," one said.

"We want to hear more," another shouted.

Metsfin nodded. "Show them the EvangeCube."

Michelle felt a brief twinge of fear, but she took the cube in her hands and held it up, just as she had the HOPE cube.

"In the beginning God created the world," she said, her voice trembling slightly. "He is holy and just. But we are sinners. We are separated from God."

The men watched her, their eyes narrowed in concentration. They were listening.

"The penalty for sin is death. But God sent His Son, Jesus, to die in our place and pay for our sins." Michelle turned through each panel as she spoke, and with every word she felt more and more at peace. Her confidence rose and her voice stopped shaking. The Holy Spirit was moving in her. It was no longer she who was speaking, and she didn't have to be afraid any more.

"This salvation is a free gift," she said. "Jesus offers it to everyone who believes in Him and accepts Him as their Lord and Savior." She gave the cube to Metsfin, and then she asked the Muslim and Orthodox men: "Would any of you like to pray to accept Jesus as your Savior?"

There was a moment of silence.

"I want to pray to Jesus," a young man near the front spoke out. Several of his friends nodded in agreement. Others behind them put up their hands or called out similar assents.

Michelle breathed out in awe. "Then let's pray," she said.

The young men bowed their heads, asking Jesus to take away their sins and come into their lives as Lord.

Metsfin was going through the group, getting names and phone numbers, when the bus finally pulled up. Michelle saw several astonished faces watching her from the windows. With a smile, she waved to them and began squeezing her way out of the crowd.

"Will you all meet back here tomorrow?" she asked. "Then we'll speak to you more." The men nodded readily.

"Bring your friends!" she called. With Metsfin behind her, Michelle walked to the bus and climbed in. Carl was there, waiting to pull her into a warm hug. She squeezed him tightly, but then pulled back with a beaming smile.

"How was it?" Dan asked her quietly.

Michelle looked towards him, her grin growing even wider. "Amazing. It…" She struggled to put words to the emotion filling her. "It feels like I'm glowing," she said finally.

Dan smiled at her. "I know the feeling."

He called to the rest of the van, above the rattle of the engine. "Let's get back to the hotel," he said, motioning for everyone to take a seat. He nodded to Michelle, a smile twitching the corners of his mouth. "Looks like you're going to have a big day of follow-up tomorrow."

For Students In Grades 9-12:

RG3: Revealing God's Greatest Glory

Like We Love Ice Cream

On the first day Michelle had visited the small village in Ethiopia, Rebecca had been one of the villagers who had instantly welcomed the gospel. She had responded joyfully to it and had become passionate about the message and about learning more. Michelle loved Rebecca dearly, even after just one day of knowing her. They shared a special bond. Michelle admired Rebecca's sweet, caring heart and her vision to reach others, and Michelle found herself partnering with Rebecca in the village ministry as the week continued.

Michelle met with the groups which she had arranged on the first day and began leading a Bible study with them. She taught them a simple, six-question Bible Study method that e3 Partners had adopted to help anyone, of any spiritual maturity, to lead an in depth Bible study. Michelle also taught them to share their faith. Afterwards the new believers would have a worship service and sing praises to God. Rebecca offered her home for the group to meet in and stayed at Michelle's side throughout the gathering. Michelle taught Rebecca how to lead Bible studies and also gave her personal training in how to share her new faith with others.

Over the course of the week, Rebecca and Michelle went all over the village sharing the gospel. Sometimes Michelle would present the gospel, other times Rebecca would. More and more people accepted Christ and joined the Bible studies and worship services. Then Michelle and Rebecca went out and found even more people. By the last day of the week, only two couples in the entire village had not yet been saved. Michelle invited them to a special celebration service which gathered all the new believers from around the village. There, Michelle shared the gospel again and had the privilege of leading both couples to Christ. The believers came together, as the four villagers knelt to pray, and laid their hands on the couples in love and support. With expressions of pure joy, the couples received forgiveness for their sins. The believers welcomed them, embracing them and laughing with them, and bringing them into the young church that had been started there in Rebecca's house.

A total of five house churches had been planted and an entire village saved, all within one week. Michelle was brimming with joy and awe. She praised God with the new congregation, blown away that God had allowed her, as scared and weak as she was, to be a part of something this amazing. She had come into this village feeling alone. She had been frightened by the Muslim and Orthodox villagers. Now she had a wonderful friend in Rebecca, and moreover, she was worshiping with the same people she had once been afraid of! It was incredible. And already her last night in Ethiopia had come.

Michelle returned to the bus and her team and drove back to get one final rest before she spent her last day in the village. After the Ethiopian believers trailed out of her house to return to their own homes, Rebecca, too, settled down to sleep. That night, as she dreamed, she had a vision of Jesus.

Michelle came back to the village the next morning, with a bittersweet realization that this would probably be the last time she ever saw these dear people. With a faint sigh, she walked up to Rebecca's house, Metsfin following quietly behind her.

As soon as Michelle came through the door, Rebecca greeted her with a warm hug. When the two friends broke apart, Michelle noticed that Rebecca seemed preoccupied by something.

"What is it?" Michelle asked. Metsfin translated for Rebecca, who only spoke Amharic.

The pauses in their conversations and Metsfin's fluid transformation of one language to another had become familiar to Michelle, until she hardly noticed it anymore.

Rebecca looked at Michelle quizzically. "I had a dream last night. Jesus...He came and spoke to me. He said..." She wrinkled her brow in concentration, trying to be sure she got the words right.

Metsfin waited for her to speak so that he could pass the message on to Michelle. But when Rebecca said what Jesus had told her, she spoke in English. Jesus had spoken to Rebecca in Michelle's language.

"'We love each other,'" Rebecca said haltingly, carefully pronouncing the English words from her dream. "'Like we love ice cream.'"

Michelle opened her mouth to speak, but for a moment she was lost for words.

Rebecca looked from Michelle to Metsfin and back again. Then, her tone curious, she asked in Amharic, "What is *ice cream*?" She said the strange English word awkwardly, unaccustomed to the way the letters sounded.

Michelle began to smile. Ice cream was her absolute favorite thing to eat, for dessert or for dinner. This message that Jesus had given was extremely particular and personal to her. *I've been here all along*, Jesus whispered in her spirit, *I know you better than you know yourself, and I've been guiding you in everything you've done.* Michelle took a deep breath to keep herself from crying. Everything God had done and everything he had shown her was starting to overwhelm her. She looked at Rebecca, who was still waiting for a response with a puzzled expression on her face.

"Ice cream is something tasty and sweet and wonderful," Michelle said. "I love it! And I love you." She hugged Rebecca again, even tighter. She would miss this precious sister terribly when she had to return home. It was a friendship she had never expected. But then again, nothing about this week had been expected.

Before the team left, they tried to help Michelle find some ice cream for Rebecca—but there wasn't any ice cream anywhere in the area. Michelle hoped that one day Rebecca would be able to taste ice cream, because then she would understand what Jesus had meant when He said: "We love each other like we love ice cream."

Freedom Behind Bars

The train rattled away along the tracks, following the curve of the hills. Dan leaned forward in his seat and looked out the window of his carriage. The glass was misty white with frost, and outside the sky looked hard and gray. As Dan watched, countryside and towns and cities flashed past the train like fast-moving pictures. He shivered slightly and burrowed further down in his coat. Dan and his team of e3 missionaries were traveling towards the Black Sea— to Kherson, Ukraine.

When the train arrived, Dan and the others bundled out into the cold. They grabbed their luggage with frozen fingers, their breath huffing white clouds into the air, and made their way to the house where they would be staying while they visited Kherson.

The very next day their ministry began at an infamous, overcrowded prison.

Carrying a box of Bibles between them, Dan and the team went to meet the warden at the front desk. He greeted them, confirmed that they were expected, and began the procedures to allow them into the prison.

"No knives, sharp objects, or anything that could be used as a weapon," the warden said. "We don't want to let the prisoners near anything that they might use to injure someone."

"Seems like a good precaution," Dan said, smiling.

The warden looked up, serious. "Yes. One-third of the people here are political prisoners,

129

one-third of them are crazy, and one-third of them are murderers."

Dan nodded uneasily and emptied his pockets with the rest of the team.

The warden checked over a few papers and then motioned that their group was free to go in. Dan picked up the box of Bibles and carried it into the prison.

Inside there were a few inmates standing around, busying themselves with projects or conversation. The prison guards led the team through the narrow halls into a large room where they would be presenting a message. As the team set up, Dan opened the box and began pulling out the Bibles. They were tied together with rope in groups of six. The knots were small and tough. Gritting his teeth Dan dug at the rope, trying to free the books and regretting the loss of his pocketknife.

"Let me help," someone said. Dan turned and saw one of the inmates standing behind him. Before he could say anything, the man took out a pair of sharp, rusty scissors and snipped effortlessly through the rope. Dan swallowed. *So much for their precautions*, he thought, watching the inmate pocket the scissors again. *Hopefully he's not a murderer. Or crazy.*

Rather nervously, Dan thanked the man and unloaded the rest of the Bibles. By this time a crowd had gathered, of both inmates and their jailers. Dan and the team said hello, introduced themselves, and then Dan began to read a story from the Bible.

The story was of Paul and Silas in prison.

"Paul and Silas had been beaten with lashes," Dan explained. "They were bleeding and in pain." The prisoners were quiet. Their attention had already been grabbed; they knew what it was like to be beaten. There were few who had escaped that experience.

"Now Paul and Silas had been put into stocks and thrown into a dark cell of the Roman prison." Dan paused. "But these men...they began singing praises to God. In pain and misery, they were able to rejoice." Dan looked out at the prisoners, shaking his head. "In my own strength, I don't think I would ever be able to sing in that situation. Would any of you?"

The prisoners thought about it, exchanging glances with their fellow inmates. They were living in a situation similar to Paul and Silas' every day, with the bad conditions of the prison. Most of them shook their heads, no—they wouldn't sing.

"No. None of us would, in our human nature." Dan opened his Bible and turned to Galatians 5. "But God's Word says that although we are in bondage in the flesh, in the Spirit we have freedom. Paul and Silas had joy to sing, even when they were beaten and in prison, because of the strength God gave them.

"But there's more," Dan continued. "Later, a great earthquake came, so powerful that it broke the doors off the cells and shattered the shackles from the prisoners' feet. The jailer came running down into the prison. He had his sword drawn, ready to kill himself, because he knew that if he lost his prisoners the Roman army would have him executed."

Dan called to the jailers who were listening from their places by the wall. "Would you get in trouble if these guys got out?"

The guards glanced around anxiously, turning pale at the thought. Obviously the answer was yes—very big trouble.

"Well, the jailer was sure that all of the prisoners had run away," Dan went on. "He raised his sword to end his life, but then—Paul and Silas stepped from the cell. They told him to stop, because all of the prisoners were still there. The jailer dropped to his knees and asked Paul and Silas, 'What must I do to be saved?'"

The crowd of inmates and jailers watched Dan intensely, as if they were the characters in the story, hanging on Paul and Silas' next words.

"Paul and Silas answered him, 'Believe on the Lord Jesus Christ, and you will be saved, you and your household.'" Dan spread his arms out to the prison room full of people. "The Lord Jesus Christ is God's Son. Because God loved the world so much, He sent His Son to die for us and to pay for the wrong things we had done. Jesus, perfect and holy, took the punishment we deserved. He was beaten for our sins. And He died—but in three days He rose again. Now that gift of redemption is free to everyone. If you accept Jesus as your Savior and ask Him to wash away your sins, you will be free in the Holy Spirit. Jesus takes away all your guilt and shame, and gives you the kind of joy and strength that let Paul and Silas sing in a jail cell."

Dan finished and allowed silence to fall for a moment, letting the gospel message reach the minds and hearts of the people. "Would any of you like to pray to receive Christ as your Savior?" he said at last.

Out of the 38 prisoners and jailers gathered in the room, 25 raised their hands to say, "Yes." Dan led them all in a prayer of salvation.

Afterwards, Dan and his team distributed the Bibles throughout the prison, and told the new Christians that a missionary would be coming soon to follow-up with them. The missionary would disciple them and have a time of Bible study each week.

Right before they had to leave, Dan got everyone to gather together for a group photograph. Dan and his team stood in front, and all the prisoners and jailers eagerly crowded in behind. As Dan stood there smiling for the camera, with the mass of prisoners pressing close behind him, he couldn't help thinking...*Where is the one with the scissors?*

Write Your Story Today

With e3 Gamelife Expeditions you can travel overseas and allow God to begin to write His story through you.

You and your parents can log on to e3partners.org to explore the many mission opportunities — you can even search by dates or country and sign up online. Expeditions last about 8 days and every expedition is a great experience. On an e3 Gamelife Expedition our trained leaders will train you to lead powerful Bible lessons using fun experiential games.

Experience an Expedition through Evangelism Outreach, Discipleship Training, and 3 Leadership Development.

Our Strategy: Reach a Child to Engage a Family to Plant a Church.

www.e3partners.org

Do You Believe the Same as Billy Graham?

One of the places where e3 Partners had been working the longest was in the country of Russia. Rick and his wife had led many teams there over the years, and they had been able to see many powerful and exciting events take place. The national coordinator in Russia was a great man of faith. God was using him in mighty ways, and large numbers of people were responding to the gospel.

Now Rick was flying into Russia yet again. The towering spires and ancient, beautiful buildings of Moscow greeted his gaze as the plane drifted lower. Rick sighed in contentment. He had grown to love this country, and in returning to it he felt welcomed and at peace.

As the airplane taxied to the gate, Rick stuck a bookmark between the pages of the book he had been reading. It was Billy Graham's newly published autobiography, entitled *Just as I Am*. His story was fascinating. While Rick was in Russia, he hoped to read a little of the book every day.

Ministry began almost at once. Rick and his team went from door-to-door sharing the gospel and saw several Russians come to faith. And every night, before he went to bed, Rick read a chapter of Billy Graham's book. The inspirational read was a wonderful conclusion to each day of outreach.

One night, while lying on his hotel bed, Rick opened the book to read. The next chapter was about a time when Billy Graham had come to Russia. Interested, Rick began reading. Billy Graham had been one of the first Christian evangelists, after Perestroika, to share the gospel on a large scale with the people of Russia. He had held several meetings in Moscow at that time, and the responses had been overwhelming. Throngs of people had come forward to profess Christ as Savior. The aisles had been packed with new believers, and people standing outside squeezed through the doors so that they, too, could show they had accepted Christ. Billy Graham had been affected strongly by what he had seen. Rick could feel it in the evangelist's words as he described the scene of rejoicing and emotion that had occurred in response to the gospel.

Rick reached the end of the chapter. He closed the book, turned off his lamp, and leaned back onto the pillow, his mind still dwelling on the story of the Holy Spirit moving in Russia.

In the morning, Rick went to an apartment complex and walked from door-to-door. At each apartment he knocked, waited for an answer, and then introduced himself as Rick, from America. "May I tell you how Jesus has changed my life?" he would ask. Sometimes no one answered the door. Sometimes they didn't really want to listen. But other times, many times, the people listened avidly. Rick was invited into several apartments and had many deep, fruitful discussions.

At one apartment, a woman came to the door in answer to Rick's knock. "Yes?" she asked pleasantly.

Rick smiled in greeting. "Hello! My name is Rick. I'm here with a team of people from America, who have come to share about our faith in God."

The woman began to stare at him. Her fingers gripped the side of her door tighter and tighter, white-knuckled. Rick noticed her reaction, but pressed on.

"May I tell you how Jesus has changed my life?" he said.

The woman barely seemed to register the question. She took a deep breath and asked, "Do you believe the same thing as Billy Graham?"

Rick blinked. "Why...y-yes, ma'am, I do."

The woman's tense features dissolved into a smile of pure joy. "You have come to tell my people about Jesus?" she said delightedly.

"Y-yes," Rick said again, confused.

"Please, come in," the woman said, opening the door to the apartment. Then she told Rick her story. Years ago, she had been at one of Billy Graham's meetings in Moscow, and she had heard the gospel and accepted Christ as her Savior. It was an amazing moment that had changed her life forever. But when she returned home from Moscow, she discovered that there were few, if any, Christians in her city. There was no church, not even a Bible study. She had no way to learn more about Christ or to grow in her knowledge and faith.

Every day since that time, she had prayed for God to send someone to her village who would bring the same message Billy Graham had taught—someone who would tell the people about Jesus and start a church in her city.

Rick listened in giddy amazement. He had been reading, just the night before, about Billy Graham's meeting in Moscow. And today he actually met someone who had been saved at that meeting? And her fervent prayer, over all those years, was for someone to come start a church in her area—something Rick and his team were striving to do? This meeting was so blatantly planned by God that Rick didn't even have to exercise his faith.

"We have been sent in answer to your prayer," Rick told the woman. "God will plant a church here."

Before Rick and his team returned to America, a church had been started in the woman's city. When the group of Russian Christians came together for their opening service, the woman was one of the first people through the door of the house. She never stopped smiling once during the meeting. After all those years, her faithful prayer had been answered. Now she had a family of believers around her and an opportunity to learn more about the God she loved—because God brought the message which Billy Graham had preached back to Russia.

God of the Storm

"You're treating me like an adult," the girl said. She sounded surprised.

Amused, Dan glanced down at the 16-year-old. "Yep."

The two stood in the airport in Sao Paulo, Brazil, waiting for their plane. The first flight, into Sao Paulo, had been an easy one. Now the team had to board another plane, a small commuter aircraft, to take them to the city where they would be doing ministry.

The girl, Erica, clasped her hands behind her and gazed around the busy airport, fascinated by the foreign sights and sounds. The rhythmic hum of a new language flowed through the air like music. Dan was pleased with how well she was adapting. He had brought a team of fifteen people down to Brazil for a mission trip, and Erica was the only teenager in the group. Despite the age difference between them, Erica conversed comfortably with her team members, and she was excited and hard-working. She would be a great asset to the team.

"Now boarding," the call came over the loudspeaker. Dan moved forward, the rest of the team getting up behind him.

After checking their seat numbers, the clerk allowed each passenger onto the plane. Only thirty people could fit onto the small aircraft, so the line was short. Fourteen of Dan's team members boarded the plane. Only Dan and Erica were left.

135

The clerk checked Dan's seat, and then looked for Erica's. He frowned. "She doesn't have a seat," he said.

Dan stepped back up to the counter. "What?" Erica looked nervous.

"She doesn't have a seat on the flight," the clerk repeated, showing Dan that all the rows were filled. "There isn't any room."

Erica's eyes flew up to Dan. "Do I need to stay here?" she asked fearfully.

"No," Dan said firmly. "You're getting on that plane."

He turned to the clerk. "You need to find another way to get my team on the plane. We can't leave Erica here."

The clerk gestured helplessly. "I really don't know what I can do. There simply aren't any seats open!"

Erica bit her lip, trying not to appear panicked. Dan prayed, leaned forward, and fixed the clerk with a steady gaze. "There are *no* seats open anywhere on the plane?"

The clerk opened his mouth to speak, but then he hesitated. "Well...there might be one seat open."

A few minutes later, Erica was sitting in the only open seat on the plane—the navigator's chair in the cockpit. The pilot watched bemusedly as the teenager buckled her seatbelt. He glanced at the clerk, who lifted his shoulders in a motion of defeat. They both turned to look at Dan, who was making sure Erica was safe and settled.

"Thank you," Dan said.

The clerk nodded, still rather flustered. Finally the pilot, too, shrugged his shoulders and turned back to the controls.

Erica couldn't stop a smile tugging at her lips as she watched the crew maneuvering around the cockpit.

"Are you all right up here?" Dan asked before he went to his seat.

"Yes, I'll be fine," Erica said excitedly, her eyes still scanning over the blinking dashboards and control panels. Dan smiled and left her to enjoy the flight.

The plane had flown for half-an-hour when turbulence began to rattle the wings. Dan pressed his face to the window and peeked out.

A gigantic storm cloud was billowing into the air directly in front of them.

Dan pulled back from the window, shocked by how quickly the clouds had appeared. Throughout the plane he heard small noises of fear and surprise from the passengers as they caught sight of the storm. Then the plane shook again, causing the anxious murmurs to rise into cries of fear.

A fork of lightning splintered the sky, flashing eerily around the interior of the plane. The plane dropped a few feet and then rose again. The air currents were shifting madly. The woman beside Dan gripped her chair arm in a death grip, staring straight ahead.

By now many of the passengers were panicking. The lightning grew more frequent, and after each strike the thunder roared through the atmosphere, pulsing like some angry drumbeat rolling off the clouds. Dan was feeling rather thrilled. To view a thunderstorm from the air was a spectacular sight—to be right in the middle of its powerful core. It was the majesty of the Creator in raw elements.

But many of the others did not feel the same exhilaration. Even the flight attendant was sitting down in a chair, shaking. Every time the plane tilted, another shade of color faded from her skin.

Dan unbuckled his seatbelt and slowly got to his feet. He moved across the tilting cabin until he could kneel beside the distraught flight attendant. She looked up at him, her eyes gleaming with fear.

"Do you know what would happen if you died today?" he asked straight off.

The woman barely seemed able to comprehend what Dan was saying. "W-what?"

Dan smiled at her, turning his tone light and jovial. "If, say, one of those lightning strikes were to hit an engine—" he pointed out the window at the flickering sky— "and this plane were to fall and hit the ground, do you know where you would spend eternity?"

The woman was taken off guard by Dan's comfortable, casual manner, and for a moment her terror lessened. "Well...I don't really know."

"Let me tell you how you can know," Dan said. "And then you will never have to fear death again."

With the plane still tossed in the hands of the gale and the thunder pounding against the windows, Dan shared the gospel with the Brazilian flight attendant. And when she had heard of Jesus' love for her and his sacrifice for her sins, she asked Dan to lead her in prayer. Together, Dan kneeling on the floor of the cabin and the woman huddled in her chair, the flight attendant prayed to the God of the storm to save her soul.

The storm eventually subsided and the pilot brought the plane safely down onto the runway. The passengers, trembling and speaking in quieter voices than normal, unbuckled their seatbelts and stumbled off the plane. The flight attendant gave Dan a faint, thankful smile as he approached her on his way out.

Dan stopped in front of her, shaking her hand warmly. "Remember, Jesus has given you eternal life," he said. "You don't need to be afraid."

Her smile grew wider. "Yes, I believe that," she said, without a quaver in her voice. Dan smiled at her and said goodbye.

He met Erica at the door of the cockpit. She was wearing a half-relieved, half-crazed grin, and her eyes seemed stuck in a perpetual state of shock.

"How was that?" Dan asked wryly.

Erica blew out a breath with an airy, nervous laugh. "Well, we made it." She looked at him resolutely, braced for whatever might be coming next.

Smiling to himself, Dan followed Erica and his team into the airport.

For Students In
Grades 10 -12:

E267: Living For Eternity

Year 3's Workbook Is In Digital Form with the Answer Key and YouTeach!

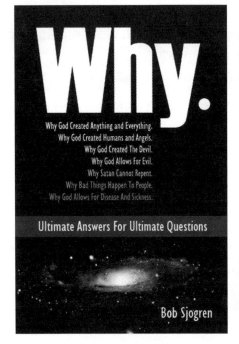

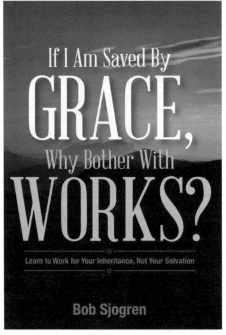

Commencement Address

Rap, rap.

Dan stepped back from the door, waiting for an answer to his knock. For several minutes he and his team stood quietly before the house—but no one came to the door.

"Another house empty," Dan said, puzzled. "Where is everyone?"

Dan and the Lithuanian Pastor Oturous, as well several others, were in Elektrėnia, Lithuania. The team had been planning to share the gospel house-to-house. But they had been walking the streets for almost half an hour now, and no one had come to their doors or been seen anywhere in the town.

Pastor Oturous pointed up the street. "Let's try over there."

The team followed him down to the next block. It was a beautiful day, the sun shining warmly and the air cool and breezy. But the quiet felt slightly eerie. Shouldn't there be other people out in the town? Why was no one around?

Rap, rap. Pastor Oturous knocked on another door. There was no answer.

"What should we do?" one of the team members asked.

"Let's go towards the town square and see if we can find anyone at all who knows what's going on," Dan said.

They hurried down the streets, their feet echoing hollowly on the cobblestones. Then, as the group moved farther into the town, the sound of voices began to rise over the housetops. At last! They hurried around the corner, eager to meet someone—anyone—who could explain where all the people were.

But when they rounded the corner, the answer was obvious.

A huge crowd of people was gathered outside an auditorium in the middle of the town, seemingly waiting to enter the front doors. All of them were talking happily and excitedly to each other. Dan and Pastor Oturous walked up to the edge of the crowd, looking on in amazement.

"What an opportunity the Lord has for us today!" Dan said. "Everyone is here in one place!"

But why? Why had all these people gathered here today?

"Excuse me," Pastor Oturous asked, gently tapping one of the men on the shoulder. "We're visitors to your town. What is happening at the auditorium?"

"Oh," the man replied cheerfully, "it is our children's school graduation day. The ceremony is inside."

Dan and Pastor Oturous looked at each other. "Wouldn't it be great," Dan said slowly, "If we could address all the children and their parents at the graduation?"

One of the team members, standing nearby, spoke up. "Surely they wouldn't allow that, though?" he asked.

"We can find out," Dan said. "Pastor, let's see if we can talk with the principal."

The rest of the team waited and prayed outside while Dan and Pastor Oturous walked into the school building. Everything was in a flurry of activity: teachers herding children into their proper places, teenagers adding the final touches to the stage, supervisors walking up and down the halls to double-check all that they could.

Dan and Pastor Oturous asked someone where they could find the principal. They were directed to a friendly-looking woman, dressed in a neat skirt, who was talking with one of her teachers.

She dismissed the teacher with a smile as Dan and Pastor Oturous walked up.

"Hello," she said. "How can I help you?"

"Hello," Dan said. "My friends and I are visiting from America. We wondered if you would allow us to share a message of hope with your children at their graduation."

The lady seemed a little surprised by the request. "Um," she said, glancing to the side, "I don't—."

Dan and Pastor Oturous silently prayed, begging God for this opportunity to share with so many people.

The principal looked at them again, studying their anxious, hopeful faces. "I think that would be fine," she said at last. "Yes, you could share a brief message."

The two men smiled delightedly. "Thank you!" they both exclaimed.

A few minutes later, all the families began to file into the auditorium and find their seats. Dan and Pastor Oturous and their small team were directed to a section of chairs where they could sit during the ceremony.

It was a fun, lively event. The children performed a variety of pieces: dancing in their traditional folk outfits, singing in choral groups, and reciting portions of poetry. The parents applauded each performance enthusiastically, and Dan's team heartily joined in.

When the official graduation ceremony was completed and the children had been seated, the principal motioned for Dan to come forward.

"We have a special guest who would like to say a few words to all of you," she said, nodding to the children. The students watched curiously as Dan came and stood beside the principal.

"Greetings from America!" he called. "We love your city and your country, and we're so glad we get to be here today. We have a message from God's Word for you. God brought us all the way from America to tell you the message found in Jeremiah 29:11: 'For I know the plans I have for you,' says the Lord, 'They are plans for good and not for evil, to give you a future and a hope.' God says that you have a future and a hope, and that future and hope can be found through a relationship with Jesus Christ."

Dan spread his hands, gesturing to all the graduated students. "This is your special day—the day the Lord has made for you. We got to listen to such wonderful songs from you today, and we wondered if we could sing something for you now—a song called, 'This Is the Day That the Lord Has Made.'"

The students cheered, laughing and clapping their hands. Dan waved for the team to join him up front. They all formed a line in front of the audience and sang a couple verses of the peppy, bouncy song: "This is the day that the Lord has made—I will rejoice and be glad in it!"

When they finished, the graduates jumped to their feet and applauded. The principal walked up beside the team, smiling. "That concludes the ceremony!" she said to the audience. "Congratulations to all our graduating classes!"

Afterwards, while the room was buzzing with the chatter of 600 excited students and all their proud, thrilled families, the principal came up and talked to Dan and Pastor Oturous.

"I really liked what you had to say," she said. "I wondered—would you come and talk to all of the teachers at my school?"

Silently, Dan thanked God for moving through his short message. "We would love to," he said, "But we are leaving Elektrėnia today. However, we will send one of our friends to come and speak to you."

Before Dan and the team left the town, they talked to a local believer and asked if he would speak with the teachers at the school. He willingly agreed.

Because of the spontaneous message at the graduation and the follow-up by the local believers, many people heard God's Word and several came to Christ. The team prayed that the youth of Elektrėnia would always remember that God loved them and had a plan for their future—and that hope was found in His Son, Jesus Christ.

Raising the funds needed for an e3 Partners expedition might sound like a scary task. For most people, it's true that "raising support" is a faith-stretching experience. However, you can be sure that if God calls you to go on Expedition, He'll provide the necessary means.

Even the Apostle Paul was financially supported. He accepted this support with enthusiasm, knowing that those who gave to his ministry were building up treasures in heaven. Paul encouraged people to give generously.

(Philippians 4:17-19)

A Strategic Photograph

Dan and a team of 78 people were going down to the Amazon River, in South America. Many of them were doctors, nurses, and dentists; they had brought supplies and equipment in order to set up medical clinics to minister to the needs of the people along the river. They had plans for a daily children's program where the kids could play games and hear Bible stories and learn about Jesus. The entire team was excited to begin. Dan was excited too. But what made this trip particularly special for him was that his wife, Lorie, and their three children, ages seven, eight, and nine, had come to South America with him.

Lorie and the kids managed the children's program. Every day, when the South American kids gathered at the team's base, Lorie and her children greeted them with friendly smiles and vibrant energy. All of the children, North and South American, quickly became friends and had a wonderful time playing games together and talking about their Bible lessons.

While the children were being ministered to in this program, the medical teams set up their clinics. People came from all around to get help for their ailments, injuries, and dental problems. When the people could not come to the clinics, the doctors and nurses and dentists climbed into boats and floated down the river to them.

There were many houses built along the banks of the Amazon. They were shabby, thatched constructions erected on stilts to keep the high flood waters from sweeping them away. Families lived in these small huts. To travel, they pushed their dugout canoes into the water and paddled up or down the river.

Dan studied a few of the odd, stick-legged cottages as he rumbled past on his motorcycle. The team had rented a few of the vehicles so that they could travel quickly along the rough dirt roads of the area. Now Dan bumped down the bank of the Amazon, enjoying the cool shade of the trees growing beside the river.

As he passed a small tributary, a gentle movement caught his eye. Dan slowly braked and brought the motorcycle to a stop. There, in the middle of the stream, was a slim, dugout canoe. A gorgeous little girl paddled quietly back-and-forth, her baby brother seated on the bottom of the canoe between her feet. The children gazed into the still water with soft brown eyes, watching the ripples from their paddle dance across the surface of the river. Dan smiled. The peaceful scene was so perfect—he had to take a picture.

Dan got off the motorcycle and pulled out his camera. As he took the picture, he heard feet running up behind him.

"Hello!" someone shouted. "Are you from the medical clinic?"

Dan turned around and saw a South American man standing in the trees a few feet away. He looked hopeful. "Can you help my son?" he asked.

Dan put the camera away. "Please, take me to him," he said, stepping through the undergrowth to the father's side. "I'll see what we can do."

The man led him to a crooked lean-to built right on the banks of the river. It was propped up, as all the houses were, on stilts. "My son fell from the lean-to ten days ago," the man explained hurriedly. "He broke his leg."

Dan followed the man inside the house. In the corner, a boy about five years old was lying on a pallet. His face was pale and his eyes were glassy with the continuous pain. Dan could see that his right leg was twisted grotesquely.

"I need to go get a doctor," Dan told the father. "I will be back as soon as I can."

The man nodded. Dan dashed from the house, leapt on his motorcycle, and tore off back to the clinic. In less than an hour, he had gathered a couple of doctors and led them back to the lean-to. The doctors moved into the house, speaking encouragingly to the family. They examined the boy's leg. It had not been set, so the child was crippled and would remain so if the break was not corrected. But after ten days, setting the leg would be extremely painful.

"Come, take his hand," the doctor said to the boy's mother. She knelt beside him, gripping the boy's hands and rubbing them between her own. The other doctors gathered around the bed, and together they moved the boy's leg back into position. The boy screamed with pain. When the bone shifted back into place he gave a great gasp and fell back on the pallet, his brow shining with sweat.

"It will be alright now," the doctor told the boy comfortingly. The doctors made a splint out of bamboo and tied the leg in place.

The boy sniffed. "It feels a little better," he said weakly. Everyone smiled.

Dan spent a good deal of time in that neighborhood. He got to know all the families who lived on the riverbank, their children, and their children's friends. The adorable little girl was a friend of the boy who had broken his leg. She shyly offered to let Dan ride in her family's canoe. Dan got a picture floating in the Amazon with the paddle wielded proudly in the air. For several days the doctors came back to check on the boy and make sure that the splint had not moved. During that time, Dan and the others were able to share the gospel with the family who lived in the lean-to, and the entire household accepted Christ.

    A year later, Dan received a picture in the mail. It was of the little lean-to on the riverbank, packed with people. The family had started a church in their home, and all the believers in that neighborhood had come to join them. Dan studied the picture fondly. A church, planted right on the shores of the Amazon River—all because a little girl and her brother were too cute not to be photographed.

For Students In
Grades 10-12:

Anticipating Heaven

Year 3's Workbook Is In Digital Form with the Answer Key and YouTeach!

146

And God Stopped the Hurricane

When the North Americans arrived in Venezuela, the nationals eagerly welcomed them. The mother church in Quibor put up a banner and sang worship songs in English and Spanish. The pastor there was a young believer named Tomas. He was a vibrant, passionate individual, and he was excited to go out and start a daughter church. The whole team was excited.

In Quibor, the North Americans and the nationals trained together in preparation for the trip to Quara. When the training program was complete and the North Americans had teamed up with their interpreters, the group was ready to set out—five national missionaries, and five of the North Americans, including Dan and his wife, Lorie.

As they began the journey, the skies started to cloud over and wind was rustling the trees. It looked as if a storm was blowing in. Dan and the others prayed that the bad weather would hold off and continued on their way.

But this gale was no ordinary thunderstorm. It was a hurricane, whirling in from the ocean across Venezuela. By the time the team arrived in Quara the sky was completely hidden. Thick clouds raced in, roiling and tumbling over themselves as the wind lashed them forwards. They growled with thunder, laden with rain—a dark, angry black. Trees bowed, creaking and groaning, as the wind rose to a howl. Like some angry beast the storm tore through the town, sending torrents of rain hurtling to the earth and forcing everyone to look for shelter.

Inside a little house, the ten believers huddled together to wait out the storm. Above them, the ceiling trembled with the force of the rain driving down upon it, and a fresh gust of wind slammed against the front door. Dan's wife looked fearfully around the house, as if wondering whether the walls could stand.

Dan squeezed Lorie's hand comfortingly. She wrapped her fingers tighter around his, and they both bowed their heads. One of the others was beginning a prayer: "Please, Father, let this hurricane stop. Let us be able to go out and share the gospel. Please keep this house safe." As long as the hurricane continued, they would be unable to share the gospel with anyone. They had arrived with such vision, but now it looked as though the trip might be for nothing.

The believers knew that God had the power to stop the storm. They had read the miraculous stories from the Bible, but they had never seen such a miracle with their own eyes. As they prayed for the rain and wind to slow, their requests seemed feeble. Would God really halt a hurricane for them?

Then Tomas, the young Venezuelan pastor, stood up. He had been a believer for a far shorter time than any of the North Americans. But he knew, as they did, that God had the power to work wonders. Tomas lifted his eyes upwards and in a strong, loud voice, recited James 5:17. "Elijah was a man with a nature like ours, and he prayed earnestly that it would not rain; and it did not rain on the land for three years and six months." His words rang out through the small house, which had suddenly fallen silent. The others were watching him, emboldened by the power of God's Word.

Five minutes passed. And in that short time, the rain ebbed, faltered, and slowly disappeared. Dan glanced up at the roof, where no drops were falling now. He smiled. God had heard the prayer of this young pastor and granted his unfaltering request. The believers talked excitedly amongst themselves, praising God for the miracle and planning how they would go out to share the Word. That day alone, as the ten missionaries went from house to house and person to person sharing the gospel, 23 people prayed to accept Christ as Savior.

Later, with the sky a clear, pale gray overhead, Dan came upon a group of 35 kids playing full-court basketball. The kids were all in their teens or early twenties, athletic and full of energy after being cooped up inside. Dan loved sports, and he couldn't resist a competitive game. He walked over and watched the game for a while. When they called a break, he asked to talk with them.

"If I play a game with you, would you listen to what my friends and I have to say?" Dan asked.

The boys considered for a moment, and then one of them replied, a slight grin on his face. "We will listen. *If* you play on every one of our teams."

Dan laughed. He agreed, and the boys welcomed him onto the court. After four games, sweat was dripping off Dan's nose and he was panting heavily, but it felt good to be out in the sun, playing a good game, and getting to know the kids better. Then came half-time.

Between breaths, Dan got the opportunity to share the gospel with the kids. They listened attentively as he explained the Good News of Christ and His sacrifice on the cross. When he had finished, he asked if any of them would like to pray to accept Jesus.

Of the 35 kids playing basketball that day, 30 of them raised their hands. Dan led them in a prayer, all the while thanking God for his continued miracles everyday—from the heavens above to the hearts of all his people on the earth.

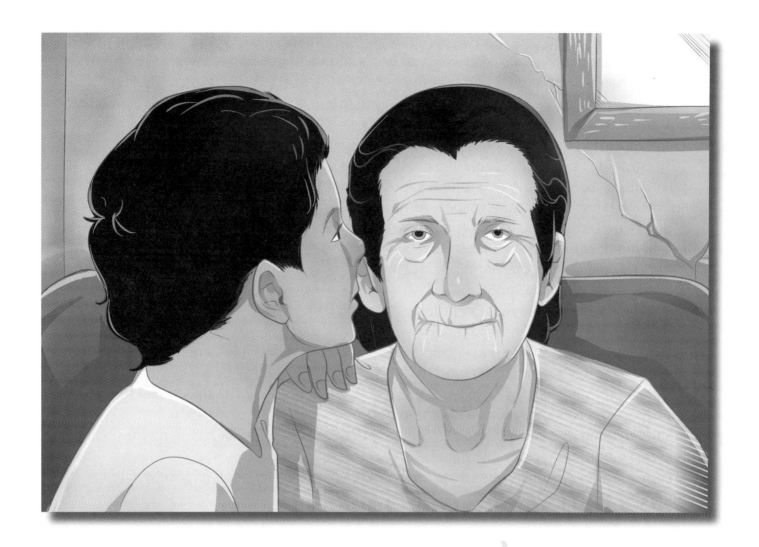

Say Yes

The next day the ground was still wet with rain, but the sun was burning bright in the clear blue sky. The weather had turned from a torrential hurricane into a hot Venezuelan summer.

Lorie walked through the town with her interpreter, her eyes narrowed against the sunlight. Lining the dirt road which they traveled, were hundreds of little homes. The children played outside, chattering and giggling, while the mothers worked indoors. Lorie had gone into several of these homes already, sharing the gospel with the families and teaching them from God's Word.

Outside one home, a small boy was playing by himself. As they approached, he caught sight of them and his face broke into a delighted grin. He scrambled to his feet, eyes wide and inquisitive, taking in the strange new spectacle of foreigners coming down his street. Lorie smiled at him and waved. He waved back, watching her walk past. Lorie felt a touch on her heart as she glanced at the boy's earnest face.

Stopping in front of his house, Lorie knelt down beside him. "What's your name?' she asked gently.

"José," he replied. Instantly he rushed on in excited Spanish.

"He wants to know why you've come," Lorie's interpreter said.

149

Lorie looked up at José. "We've come to tell you about Jesus. Would you like to hear?"

The boy nodded vigorously. He seized Lorie's hand and pulled her towards the house, yammering happily. Lorie ducked inside the hut, blinking to adjust her eyes to the dim light. There were only a couple pieces of furniture in the room, but in one rickety chair by the corner an old woman was sitting quietly. José dropped Lorie's hand and ran over to the woman. He reverently touched her knee, looking up at her adoringly. "Abuela," he said to Lorie. *Grandma*.

The grandmother rested a gnarled hand on José's head, smiling at him.

Lorie took a seat on the floor and when José and his grandmother had both turned to listen, she began to present the gospel. José leaned forwards, drawn in by every word, his gaze fixed on Lorie's face. In the background his grandmother watched silently. Her features were worn and lined; Lorie could not read what was going on in her mind.

At the end of Lorie's presentation, José was sitting as close to her as he could. He watched her eagerly as if hoping for more.

"Would you like to pray to accept Jesus?" Lorie asked.

José nodded. "Sí, sí!" he said fervently.

Lorie led him in a simple prayer, and the little boy bowed his head and prayed that Jesus would take away his sins and come into his life as Lord. When José lifted his eyes, a new energy was coursing through his body. He leapt to his feet, laughing and grinning, unable to stay still. He ran across the room, straight to his grandmother.

Suddenly the boy quieted. He carefully climbed up beside her, perching on the chair arm, and put his mouth to her ear. "Sí, Abuela," he whispered. "Sí."

Lorie didn't need an interpreter to understand what was happening. José was telling his grandmother to say yes to Jesus.

A single tear ran down the old woman's face. She gripped José's hands tightly and turned towards Lorie. "Sí," she said softly.

Lorie went to the old woman's chair, her own eyes suddenly burning. "May I pray with you?"

With José clinging to her arm, the grandmother, too, bowed her head and accepted Jesus.

When Lorie left, José gave her a huge hug. "Gracias," he said, his dirt-smudged face trapped in a radiant smile. He looked up at his grandmother who was standing at his shoulder. The old woman put her arm around her grandson and smiled.

Lorie learned again a lesson God had shown her before: the effect of a mission to reach children does not stop there. Once the children know about Jesus' love and salvation, they turn and tell their families about Christ—even a little boy just a few seconds old in the Lord.

A Way In

"Dan, we have a job for you," one of the e3 leaders said. "We want to take another team to Cuba, and I'd like you to lead it. But our last missionary group was forced to leave. We need to find a covert way to get into Cuba through Mexico." He paused. "Any ideas?"

Dan was silent for a moment; then he nodded, and started to grin. "Maybe."

The team was leaving soon, and Dan didn't have much time to strategize. They were already planning to bring in bags of medical supplies to deliver as part of their cover for coming to Cuba. Dan thought this over and hit upon a brilliant plan.

The next day, Dan approached the team, wearing a broad smile. "Congratulations! You are all now tourists on a grand adventure into Cuba." He handed out handfuls of luggage tags and tourist badges to all of the team members, who accepted them with looks of confusion.

One of them, a man named Kevin, looked down at his badge with a frown. "Love and Mercy Fun Tours?"

"We're not just any tour. We have love, mercy, and fun, and we really want to get to know the people and help them out. How do you like our logo?" Dan asked.

The team looked at each other, and then started to smile.

"I hope this works," one said.

"Me too," Dan agreed heartily.

When the team landed in Cuba, they faced their first big obstacle—immigration. The Americans split up, trying to avoid each other, not make eye contact, and do everything possible to not look like a group. One of their partners, Ramon, was supposed to meet them at immigration and take care of all the official business. Ramon had come down to Cuba earlier, and Dan was trusting that he had everything worked out.

The new arrivals were crowded inside a circle, where the officials had to check each passenger through before they could cross to where their family and friends were waiting. Dan caught sight of a few of his team members out of the corner of his eye, scattered amongst the people. They were all waiting silently. Then Dan saw the officials coming around and asking each person for something. In response, the new arrivals would pull out some slips of paper and hand them to the officials; the officials would check the papers and then wave the passengers out into the waiting crowd. Dan barely had time to worry before one of the officials, a rough, stern-faced woman, was asking him for his hotel vouchers.

Dan looked blankly at her. "My...hotel vouchers?" Ramon had said nothing about this. He hadn't given them anything.

"Do you have them?" she said impatiently.

Glancing over the woman's shoulder, Dan saw several of his other team members being talked to, and saw their equally startled faces as they realized they had nothing to show.

"Stand over here, please," the woman said shortly. Dan moved to the side, wondering what he could possibly do.

Everyone who didn't have a hotel voucher was directed off to the side. Despite all their efforts to stay separated, Dan's whole team was promptly weeded out and forced to stand in a huddle. A few of them looked to Dan, as if expecting he would have an idea of what to do.

The woman was walking over now, glaring at them. The officers had checked everyone else, and now only Dan and his friends were left inside the circle. One of the other officials was nearby, and the woman waved him over. The team was beginning to look nervous. Cuba was a visibly communist country at this time, and many of the officials were carrying machine guns.

Dan watched the immigration officers talking, and it soon became clear that they wanted to send them back on the very plane on which they had come. Dan knew he had to do something quickly, or they would be heading back to America before Ramon even showed up.

"Excuse me!" Dan said, walking over to the officials. "My friend Ramon is supposed to meet us here. I'm sure he has the hotel vouchers. Would you allow me to go and look for him?"

The woman grudgingly agreed. Dan hurried off to the edge of the circle, searching the crowd frantically for a glimpse of Ramon. But there was nothing. Not knowing what else to do, Dan cupped his hands around his mouth and shouted, "Ramon!" The whole crowd started staring at him. "Ramon!" Dan shouted again, painfully aware of how ridiculous he looked, and feeling the blazing stare of the woman on the back of his head. He prayed that Ramon would show up soon. He continued shouting, worried that if he stopped or even looked back at the official, she would tell him to step away from the line and that would be the end of their trip to Cuba.

For fifteen excruciating minutes Dan shouted, and then, blessedly, he heard a voice shouting back, "Dan! Dan!"

Ramon struggled through the crowd, beaming and waving. Dan breathed a huge sigh of relief.

It turned out Ramon didn't have the vouchers either. But he talked with the officials and persuaded them to let Dan and his team through. Then came the next challenge—their bags had to make it past customs. There were some bags filled with medical supplies, which matched their cover story of Love and Mercy Fun Tours, but there were also bags of Bibles. Suspicion had already been aroused towards their group, which made it even less likely that any of the luggage would go unchecked.

Dan and the others prayed that the officers would only open the bags of medical supplies. After several long moments of breathless waiting, they received the clearance to leave customs with all of their suitcases—the officers had only checked the medical supplies! Giving praise to God, the team was at last free to enter Cuba.

Two Prayers, One Answer

God had surmounted the first and largest difficulty of getting into Cuba—immigration. Now the team could begin their ministry there. Everyone got a night's rest, and the next day the team started off to visit the mother church with which they were partnering.

After a weary journey, Dan and the team arrived at the church and attended a service. Their worship was led by a lone guitarist—if the instrument he strummed could be called a guitar. There was a gaping hole broken into its body and only one string stretched along the neck. How he could produce any music at all was a miracle, but the congregation sang out lustily and cheerfully.

Kevin, one of the members of Dan's team, couldn't bear watching the guitarist strum on his solo string. He hurried over to Dan, his face lined with concern. "Dan, we have to get them a guitar!"

Dan took one look at Kevin and said, "Yep, we have to get them a guitar."

But where could they find a guitar in Cuba? The average salary was a dollar a day. The shops and shelves were practically barren, and the countryside itself was a desolate, tough, poverty-stricken place. Finding such an instrument could only come from God.

After a full day at the mother church, the team headed back to where they were staying.

However the cars had no headlights, and when darkness fell they were driving by moonlight, trying their best to avoid all the gigantic potholes in the road. Finally they arrived safely and tumbled into bed.

The next morning Dan's team was on their way to the mother church when Dan suddenly remembered—they had to find a guitar. He pulled their car over to the side of the road and prayed simply, "Lord, we need a guitar. You know where there is a guitar. Please show us where that is."

Dan pulled back onto the road. "You know," he said suddenly, "I think we should turn here."

"Why?" asked Kevin.

"I have no idea," Dan said, steering the car onto a bumpy side road.

The team was quiet as the car rolled along, heading farther into territory they had never seen before. With a lurch, Dan took another right, and headed determinedly on. After a while, they found themselves entering a small town. Dan drove to the square and stopped the car. It was a fairly quiet place, but there were a good number of homes and a few shops were close by.

Dan exchanged glances with his team, and they all piled out into the hot, dusty morning. He led the way into the first store, his hopes building.

"Would you happen to have a guitar?" Dan asked the manager in broken Spanish.

He stared at Dan for a moment, and then burst out laughing.

The next shop was no better.

"You won't have any luck finding a guitar around here," the clerk said, smiling and shaking his head.

At that moment a man walked past outside, carrying a guitar on his back.

"Ha!" Dan shouted, as the team nearly fell over themselves to get out the door.

"Senór," Dan said, panting. "Would you be interested in selling us your guitar?"

The man looked shocked. "Oh, no! It is my livelihood! I am a concert guitarist, and I play in the orchestra! I teach lessons...I couldn't possibly part with my guitar." He paused. "But I do know someone who is trying to sell theirs."

"Can you take us to them?" Dan exclaimed.

"Sure," the man shrugged.

They all clambered into the van, squeezing the guitarist inside, and drove off. Fourteen blocks away the man motioned for them to stop outside a small house. Dan and the team walked up to the front door, knocked, and waited. A family came to the door.

"Can we buy your guitar?" Kevin asked.

All of the family were believers in Christ. They were very poor, and they had been praying desperately for God to sell their guitar at the same time that Dan had been praying to buy one. The family was overjoyed, and Dan and the team overpaid generously for the instrument.

Dan thanked the family and the guitarist, and everyone packed back into the van—plus one guitar. They found their way back to the main road and headed to the church, where Kevin was able to present the new, whole, five-stringed guitar to the ecstatic worship leader. God's plans had been intricately laid; it was just another reminder that He had everything under control, even when it came to finding a guitar.

At the Right Time

A mother and a daughter walked down the long, sunny street in Cuba. Their names were Lisa and Britney. The girl was eighteen years old. They had come from America to share the gospel with the people in Cuba, but at the time, Cuba was a Communist country— there were restrictions on sharing the gospel.

Their team leader, Rick, had assigned teams of two people to each side of each street in the neighborhood they were visiting. Lisa and Britney were to walk down their roadside, going from house-to-house. If the people who answered the door wanted to hear about Jesus and invited them in, they could share the gospel there, indoors and in private. But Lisa and Britney couldn't talk to anyone out on the street. And they weren't supposed to cross the street.

Britney knew this. So her mother was surprised when Britney suddenly stopped walking and said, "Mom, we need to go to that house across the street."

Her mother looked at her in confusion. "Honey, this is our side. We are assigned here. We're not supposed to go across."

Britney turned to her mother, her voice strained with urgency. "You don't understand. We *have* to. God told me I have to go to that house."

Lisa looked out over the road. She could see the other team knocking at a house just a few doors down from the one her daughter was talking about. "But Britney," she tried to reason with her, "Our other team members will be there in good time. They can take the gospel to that house."

Britney shifted back and forth on the pavement, her hands trembling with nervous energy. "Mom, I..." she glanced at the house, and then back at her mother. For a moment she hesitated. "I'm sorry, Mom," she blurted out, "but I have to go. God says 'Go to that house *now*!' You can come or you can stay, but *I* need to cross the street."

Britney turned and hurried out into the road. Lisa started to call after her, but she knew her daughter well, and she had seen that look in her eyes. Britney was serious. Sighing softly, Lisa jogged after her daughter.

She caught up with Britney across the street. Britney smiled, relieved that her mom had decided to come. Lisa returned the smile, but all the while she wondered what could have gotten into her daughter.

Together they approached the house, went up to the door, and Britney raised her hand to knock. She paused just a moment to take a deep breath, and then she pounded sharply on the door.

There was a long silence. Britney looked down at her shoes, up at her mother, and back to the door. She was still staring at the doorjamb when she heard a lock being turned. With a creak the door was inched open, and a pale, worn-faced man looked out at them. He seemed dazed, and his eyes were distant, as if focused on something very far away.

"Hello, sir!" Britney said.

The man looked down at her, still wearing the same look of shock and confusion.

"We've come to share the Good News. Would you like to hear about Jesus?" Britney asked.

The man was silent for a moment, and then he gave his head a little shake, as if trying to wake himself up. "Please," he said hoarsely. "Come in. You came at just the right time."

Britney and Lisa glanced at each other. They followed the man into the house, where he seated them across from himself and waited, listening.

Britney began by sharing her testimony, and how Jesus had changed her life. Lisa followed, and then Britney told the man the gospel.

"Jesus is God's Son. He came to earth to die for all the wrong things we did, so that we wouldn't have to pay that penalty. If anyone trusts in Jesus as their Savior and accepts Him as Lord, He forgives all their sins and promises them eternal life in heaven with God. It is a free gift. We can never earn it, and we don't have to. Jesus has done everything already. All we have to do is receive it," Britney finished. She paused, watching the man's face. He had his head lowered, and his hands were clasping and unclasping anxiously.

"Sir," Britney said softly. "Would you like to pray to Jesus? Would you like to be saved?"

The man raised his eyes; they were glowing with tears. "Yes," he whispered. He turned his head and wiped his eyes dry. "Yes, please, Jesus...You came at the right time...You came at the right time..."

He began to sob. Britney and Lisa went over to him and led him in prayer. Through his tears, the man prayed to Jesus and asked Him to forgive his sins and save him. When he had finished, he was still crying. But now he was smiling, too.

Britney and Lisa invited the man to come to the first meeting of believers in that town, being held that evening. The man came and participated enthusiastically in the worship of his Savior and the study of the Bible, which he had never read before. Afterwards, Britney and her mother went to him and began talking with him. The man's whole countenance had changed. He chatted amiably with them, and there was always a smile hovering on his lips. A fierce joy was within him that seemed to radiate like a bright light.

"I wanted to ask you something," Britney said at last. "What did you mean when you kept saying, 'You came at the right time'?"

The man's face became sober. "When you knocked on my door, I was out in the backyard with a gun to my head, about to end my life."

Britney felt her heart turn cold. Stunned, she listened as the man continued.

"If you had not, at that exact moment, come to my house, I would have pulled the trigger and been dead." He smiled solemnly. "But God was merciful. You came, and you brought the gospel to me. And now I am free."

Britney turned slowly to her mother. She could think of nothing to say. Both of them were wrestling with the gravity of what they had heard. If they had waited for the other team members to reach the man's house, it would have been too late. If Britney hadn't listened to the voice of the Holy Spirit and gone off their assigned path, the man would now be entering eternity without a knowledge of God—instead of rejoicing now with the believers in his new hope in Christ.

Midnight Miracle

It was growing dark outside; a rosy glow in the milky clouds was all that remained of the sun. But as the twilight settled, the light within the hotel room pulsed brighter and brighter. Jim Clark and his fellow team members were too excited to go to bed. They were all sitting together in the hotel room, talking with the national Christian leader who was the e3 Partners' coordinator here in Cuba. With many smiles and eager gestures, they told their stories of what God had done that day in their ministry. Their lively discussion went on late into the night until finally the team started to break up to head off to bed, yawning and saying good nights.

"We'll give you a lift home," Jim told the national coordinator as he stood to leave. Like most of the people in Cuba, the man didn't own a car. Normally he would either wait at the side of the road for someone to give him a ride or he would walk back to his village. Of course, Jim and his friend wouldn't hear of such a thing. They were only too happy to drive him home.

All the way there they talked animatedly, and when Jim pulled up outside the coordinator's house, none of them wanted to leave just yet. It was now a little after midnight. Jim parked the car, and with only the air conditioning blowing gently, the three men continued their talk. They spoke about plans for the morning: when and where they would meet and their strategies for sharing the gospel.

Rap! Rap!

Jim jumped, startled by the violent knock on the car window. He looked out and saw a police officer standing next to the car, hands-on-hips and glowering fiercely. Jim was nervous as he rolled the window down.

"I'm sorry, sir," Jim said politely, "Is there a problem?"

The man's chest expanded with rage. "You are making too much noise! It is after midnight, and you are here disturbing the neighbors, upsetting the peace and quiet!"

Jim was shocked into silence, his heart pounding aggressively. He hadn't meant to do anything wrong. The car's lights were off. The windows were rolled up. Jim and his friends had been talking quietly. How could the officer have even heard them from outside of the car? And why was he so angry over what seemed such a minor incident?

The situation felt wrong. Jim had an unsettling sense of *something else* being involved in the confrontation. Was this opposition from more than just an irritated officer?

For our struggle is not against flesh and blood, Jim remembered.

The policeman continued to rant, yelling non-stop accusations in Jim's face, every line of his body taut with wrath. Jim began praying silently, "Lord, bind Satan in the Name of Jesus Christ, and make him flee from this place."

As he was still praying, the policeman stopped yelling.

In the peaceful quiet that followed, the officer lifted his eyes and refocused on Jim. A huge smile broke across his face. "Good evening, sir!" the man said exuberantly, as if greeting him for the first time.

Jim stared. Behind him he felt his friend and the coordinator leaning forward for a better look, wondering whether this was still the same policeman.

The officer began chatting happily with Jim, laughing merrily and even reaching into the car and patting him on the shoulder. Then, grinning, the man tipped his hat and said, "Have a great night, sirs," and walked away down the road.

The policeman had gone from screaming to laughing to saying a cheerful good bye in a matter of seconds.

Jim watched the officer in the rearview mirror, aware of the swelling silence filling the car. The coordinator and team member looked at each other in confusion.

"And...what just happened?" Jim's friend prodded.

Jim lifted his shoulders in an expression of awe and disbelief. "I asked God to rebuke Satan...and He did."

The coordinator smiled. Jim's friend grinned and shook his head in amazement. "You know, for a moment there I thought he was going to arrest us," he said.

Jim gripped the lifeless steering wheel, gazing out into the darkness once more. The police officer was nothing more than a spot in the distance, still steadily moving away.

"Well," Jim said at last, "At this rate we'll be here all night."

He unlocked the car doors, telling the coordinator to hurry home and get some rest. "We've got another big day tomorrow," Jim said with a smile.

On the way back to the hotel, Jim had a strong sense of the presence of God. He was a man unaccustomed to miracles, and to see God answer his prayer in this way was a comfort and a blessing to him. *God is near, always*, Jim reminded himself. *He showed that today. He is always waiting to support and provide, if we will only ask in faith.*

A Chess Game, the Gospel, and the King

When Jesus taught, he often used illustrations. He would take something that the people knew well, something that was common in their culture, and use it to help them understand spiritual truths—like when Jesus used the mustard seed to show how just a little faith can accomplish great things.

Jesus was, of course, the greatest teacher ever to walk the earth. So if people wanted to help others understand truths about God, it made sense to imitate this strategy. Consequently Dan taught his teams of missionaries to take ordinary, everyday objects from the cultures of the countries they visited, pray for God's wisdom, and see how God would use it to make Himself known.

Dan and a team with e3 Partners were on a mission trip to Cuba. They had several days to simply walk through the streets and share the gospel. There were many people in the town and only so many they could reach in the time that they had. So the team prayed: "Lord, direct our steps today. Take us to the people You have prepared for us to meet." Each person squeezed the hands of the teammates next to them. "Amen."

The team split into pairs and began to divide up throughout the town. It was a warm, peaceful day. The streets were quiet; even the noise of the children playing sounded distant and muted. Above their heads the round, golden sun slowly melted a hole in the azure sky.

Dan and his close friend, Ben, walked together down a narrow alleyway. They talked a little, but the atmosphere soon lulled them into companionable silence. As they strolled casually past the houses and small buildings, they listened for the Holy Spirit's prompting, looking around for anyone who seemed open to hear God's message.

Within a few minutes, Dan and Ben came upon a group of three young men. They were sitting on the ground outside a house with an old chessboard balanced between them. One of the young men was rubbing his hands together in intense concentration, narrowing his eyes to examine the pieces scattered across the board. Dan and Ben walked up to them.

"Hello," Dan said. "My friend and I are visiting from America. My name is Dan, and this is Ben."

The young men stopped their game and got to their feet, shaking Dan's hand heartily and greeting Ben with brilliant smiles. Dan moved over to look down at the chessboard. He felt a thought stirring in the back of his mind. "Lord, show me how You can use this for Your glory," he prayed quietly.

"You have quite a game going," Dan said cheerfully. "You know, life is a lot like a chess game."

The young men stood around Dan, mildly curious. "We all make our moves, but we never know exactly what is going to happen," Dan said, gesturing towards the pieces. He turned to the chess players with a smile. "Wouldn't it be great to know exactly what your opponent was going to do next?"

The young men began to grin.

"You'd win every time!" Dan said. They laughed, nodding in agreement. "Well, God is like a master chess player. He knows everything that is going to happen. And He's given us the Bible, to tell us how we can go through life and make the right choices." The young men gathered closer, their expressions remaining open and interested.

Dan, Ben and the chess players each took a seat around the board. "The ivory pieces represent the kingdom of God," Ben said all at once. Dan glanced at him, surprised. It appeared that Ben, too, had seen an illustration in the chess board.

"The dark pieces are mankind." Ben traced a line on the board. "And this line here—the line that the black pieces can't cross—represents sin. Sin separates us from God and his kingdom. No black piece can cross over into the white side."

Dan smiled. Ben had pulled out a wonderful image. "May I clear the board?' he asked.

The young men nodded, now more interested in what these men had to say than in the game that had absorbed them a few minutes earlier.

Dan swept all the pieces off into his lap, and then replaced four onto the board—one ivory and three dark. "The ivory piece is God's Son, Jesus," Dan said, setting the ivory king on one side of the line. "He is the only one who could pay the price that our sins deserve." He placed the three black pieces on the other side of the line.

"Jesus came to earth as a man and died on the cross to take the punishment for us," Dan explained. He took the ivory king and slid it across the line, over to where the dark pieces were. "Three days later He rose again. And if anyone believes in Jesus Christ and puts his trust in Him, Jesus cleanses them from all their sins and makes them as clean as new fallen snow."

Dan took one of the dark pieces and swapped it out for an ivory one. "Then that person can cross over to God, free from sin and darkness."

Dan reset the board with three dark pieces and the one ivory king. "Now, those three pieces are you three."

The young men looked up at Dan, eyes wide. "You have the ability to choose Jesus and have your sins washed clean. All you have to do is accept His gift." Dan spread his hands over the chess board. "Just as that dark piece was exchanged for ivory, your sins can be exchanged for righteousness."

When Dan finished speaking, the tranquil stillness flowed back in. The young chess players sat quietly, thinking through everything Dan had said.

One young man, the tallest of the three, bent over the chessboard, staring at the three dark pieces balanced on the edge of victory. He reached out and took up the piece that represented his life.

Then the young Cuban moved the piece up to the line where the ivory king waited.

"Yes," he said. The young man turned and met Dan's eyes, his face glowing. "I want to accept Jesus."

While his two friends watched, with Dan and Ben kneeling at his side, the man prayed for Jesus to take away his sins. Dan rested his hand on the young man's shoulder and smiled as a new believer was welcomed into the kingdom of God.

His two friends were not yet ready to make a decision. But Dan and Ben left Bibles and some Christian books for them, which they promised to read. The man who had accepted Christ thanked Dan and Ben profusely, clutching his own, new Bible tightly in his hands. Dan and Ben prayed over him, and at last they bid the three friends farewell. Even though the two might not have accepted Christ that day, now their friend would be a witness to them. And certainly, every time they played chess from that day onward, they would remember how Jesus stands at the line, ready to bring them over from darkness into light.

The Most Important Thing Ever

God had given Lorie Hitzhusen a vision to begin a ministry for children. E3 Partners had many great outreaches, but few specifically targeted kids. Lorie hoped to change that. On their next mission trip, Dan and Lorie went to Cuba to see if a children's program could be started there. Then, if that strategy worked, they planned to take the children's ministry all over the world.

On the first day in Cuba there was a downpour. The team couldn't go out into the field, so they gathered with the nationals for a day of training. This gave the Americans time to get to know their interpreters and the nationals with whom they would be partnering.

There was one lady with whom Lorie immediately felt a kinship. From across the room their eyes met, and the lady smiled a warm, beautiful smile. Right away, Lorie knew that she wanted to be friends with this lady. They couldn't even communicate, as they each spoke a different language, but both ladies already felt close.

With the help of an interpreter, Lorie introduced herself to the lady. She responded in kind. Her name was Dailenys, and she was the children's director for the local church. Lorie looked at her, astonished. There was already a children's ministry here? Dailenys explained that e3 Partners' Venezuelan director, who had gone on a trip with Dan to India, had come to their church and trained them in *I Am Second* groups—a Bible study tool taught by e3 Partners. Dailenys had taken that same curriculum and adapted it for the children. She was teaching two ladies from other churches to lead their own children's programs as well.

It was incredible. Dailenys had done the very thing that Dan and Lorie were seeking to begin. Her program was thriving and already beginning to multiply! Lorie asked Dailenys if she could watch how she ran her ministry. If Lorie could learn the strategy, she could then work to start the same kind of program in other countries.

For several days Lorie shadowed Dailenys as she held her youth program. The meeting was in the afternoon. In the morning, as the team of missionaries went from house to house, Lorie and Dailenys invited every child they met to come to the afternoon program. Their goal for the week was to be able to witness to the children's families and to teach the children who had accepted Christ how to share their faith.

About 30 or 40 kids showed up at the first meeting, including the children who were already regular attendees. When they were all gathered, Dailenys would sit down with them and tell a Bible story. One little boy, a five-year-old named Ricky, inched close to Dailenys and grasped her arm. He stared up at her with wide, hungry eyes as she told the stories of Jesus healing the sick. The next day was just the same. He couldn't get enough of God's Word.

Lorie loved little Ricky from the moment she first met him. He was a smart child with a passionate, loving heart. Dailenys told her that he came from a home where the stepfather was abusive to his mother. He had an older brother as well as a younger brother, who was only one month old. "Ricky is sweet and enthusiastic," Dailenys said. She dropped her voice to a whisper. "He is one of my favorites," she said with a smile.

On the third day, Dailenys taught the children about the EvangeCube. Lorie picked one up and sat next to Ricky. Her interpreter came over and helped Lorie talk with Ricky and show him how to share the gospel using the cube. Ricky was terribly excited. His brows furrowed in concentration, he turned through each panel and shared the pieces of the gospel in his five-year-old Spanish. When he finished each panel, the interpreter looked back at Lorie and nodded. Yes, he was doing it right!

Lorie watched little Ricky go through the cube again and again, his face growing more thrilled by the minute. He practiced sharing the gospel as passionately as if he were talking to a dear friend. It was the sweetest thing Lorie had ever seen.

Soon it was time for Lorie and Dailenys to go out into the field and share the gospel. When Ricky heard, he leapt to his feet and grabbed Lorie's hand. "Come to my mama's house," he pleaded. "Come, come!" He dragged Lorie and Dailenys the short distance from the youth program to his house.

It was a small one-room house with dirty curtains for a door. Ricky dropped Lorie's hand as they reached the entrance and sped inside, laughing. Dailenys led the way through the curtains with Lorie behind her.

Inside, Ricky was sitting on the bed beside his mother, who was holding his one-month-old brother. Ricky patted his brother's head and grinned at Lorie. Dailenys spoke with his mother in Spanish, introducing them and explaining why they were there. While they conversed, Lorie stood in the background, watching Ricky. He rocked back and forth on the bed, still wearing his delighted, playful smile.

"We may sit down now," Dailenys told Lorie. They sat on the floor in front of Ricky's mother, and Lorie shared her testimony. Then Dailenys and Ricky's mother talked a bit more in Spanish. Finally Dailenys said that they could now share the gospel.

Lorie and Dailenys looked at each other for a moment, and then they both smiled. "Let's have Ricky do it," they said.

Lorie handed Ricky the EvangeCube and he took it in his little hands with a wriggle of joy. Instantly he began sharing with his mother. Ricky turned carefully to the first panel and explained the first piece of the gospel; when he had finished the section, he spun around to look at Lorie and Dailenys. "Am I doing it right?" he piped, his eyes sparkling.

"Yes! Yes, you are," Dailenys encouraged him. He flashed a grin and turned back to the EvangeCube.

Ricky went through the entire cube, constantly checking with Dailenys and Lorie. When he finished, his mother smiled at him. She wasn't ready to make a decision yet, but she was proud of her little boy for all that he had learned.

Then Lorie and Dailenys got ready to visit the next house. Without hesitation Ricky jumped off the bed and followed them out the door. As they approached his neighbor's house, he grabbed Lorie and Dailenys's hands and looked up at them. "This is the most important thing ever," he said solemnly. "I have to tell everyone."

Lorie felt goose bumps cover her arms. "You're right," she said. "It is the most important thing."

Ricky begged them to let him share the EvangeCube at the neighbor's house. Of course they allowed him to, and Ricky stayed with Lorie and Dailenys the entire day, sharing the gospel at every house they visited. "Can I share now?" he would ask quietly, as the adults talked. "Can I share now?" Every time he got to hold the EvangeCube, he nearly burst with eagerness.

Lorie and Dailenys visited one house where the family was already saved, but Ricky, not understanding, danced up and down excitedly. "Can I tell them now?" he asked.

They laughed, and Lorie explained. "They already know Jesus," she said, "but you can share again!"

Lorie was touched deeply by this little one's faith. She never forgot the precious look on Ricky's face and his joy as he shared the gospel. Ricky had an understanding that most adults did not possess. Knowing Jesus was truly the greatest thing in the world, and the most important thing that any believer could do was to tell as many people as possible.

Join us. Let these stories become your stories and experience the joy of revealing God's glory.

Down the Jungle Path

Seven people were packed into the small rental car as Jim Clark guided the vehicle down a long, winding road, following directions from the national e3 Partners coordinator who was sitting in the front passenger seat. Jim and a team of five others were in Cuba doing ministry. Every day, in the company of the Cuban coordinator, they traveled to a different village to share the gospel. Most of the places they visited were remote communities back in the bush and required a significant amount of bumping and rattling about in the car to reach.

Earlier that morning, the coordinator had gone to visit a village some distance out in the jungle. He had contacted the family who hosted the village's house church and had told them that a group of Americans would be coming. The family received the news excitedly. Now, as Jim and the others drove towards the village, the family was busily preparing their house for a church service and inviting their neighbors to attend.

"Which way?" Jim asked, keeping his eyes on the road.

The national coordinator pointed off to the right. "Up here. If you turn off on this path here, it will take you back to the village."

Jim frowned. "What path?"

As the car rolled closer, Jim saw what appeared to be a footpath, barely distinguishable in the grass—definitely not a road. *Well, it isn't my car*, Jim thought. He turned the wheel and pressed down on the accelerator. With a heave, the car rocked onto the grass and began its slow, jolting progress into the bush.

They drove far away from any main roads, deeper and deeper into isolated territory. Eventually the path turned into the jungle. The trees got thicker, casting their shadows across the little car as it picked its way over the roots and leaves. Jim winced as the tires hit a particularly pronounced root.

"How much farther is it?" he asked.

The national e3 coordinator was leaning forward in his seat, peering out through the windshield. "Not much farther...yes!" he pointed forward. "There it is, up ahead."

Jim drove into a small clearing and found himself on the edge of a village. Many houses, constructed of wood and thatch, sat clustered together in the midst of the jungle. Jim parked the car and everyone climbed stiffly out, their limbs cramped from being packed in so tightly.

"Come on," the national coordinator called, striding energetically into the village. "Follow me!"

Jim and the others walked after him. He led them to a house near the center of the village where an assortment of benches and chairs had been set up in the front yard. A small crowd of Cubans were gathered, mostly neighbors and friends of the family who hosted the church. As the Americans arrived, the family came forward to greet them.

"Thank you for coming," the father said, grinning. "It is a great blessing to have you here."

His child echoed the sentiments, looking at the visitors with friendly curiosity. The wife, also, welcomed Jim and his friends pleasantly. But she couldn't seem to stop staring at Jim. Almost subconsciously, her eyes kept traveling towards him, a look of awe and disbelief on her face. Jim couldn't understand why she would look at him so.

"We will begin the service soon," the husband said. "We've set up chairs for you."

Jim and his teammates seated themselves, and within a few moments worship began. It stirred Jim's heart to praise God with these people, beneath the canopy of the jungle, with the trees and thatched huts all around. Then Jim, who had been asked to give the message, stood up. Several of the Cubans at the service were not saved, and Jim had the privilege of sharing the gospel with them using the EvangeCube.

All throughout the service, during the songs and the message, the wife of the house kept staring at Jim. Jim was starting to get a little uncomfortable. Finally, after the service ended and the people were milling about visiting, Jim went up to her.

They talked for a few minutes about the service, the village, and Jim's team. Still the woman's eyes kept jumping up to Jim's face, with that same scrutinizing gaze.

"Is there a reason you keep looking at me?" Jim asked at last. "Is my shirt on inside out or something?"

The woman looked startled, and then she laughed softly. "No—I'm sorry. It's just…I had been praying for someone to come to our village and teach. Last night I had a vision, and God told me that my prayer would be answered the very next day—that an American would come and preach at my home."

Jim tried not to betray the shock on his features. She had had a vision about *him*?

"Then, early this morning, my friend—" she gestured to the national coordinator, "came and told us that someone would be coming to speak at our church service." She smiled. "I was astounded. And, just as God promised, you and your team came and preached. So I am sorry—that is why I keep staring at you. You are the answer to my prayers."

Jim grinned in spite of himself. He had certainly never heard that statement applied to himself before! "Thank you for sharing with me," he said.

Jim left the woman to visit with her neighbors, struggling to comprehend what he had just heard. It wasn't every day that you met someone who had had a dream from God about something you were going to do! He shook his head in amazement.

Later in the day, with the house church as their starting point, Jim and his team went throughout the rest of the village. From house-to-house they shared the knowledge of God and salvation, and the team saw several more people come to faith in Christ. The next time the house church met, they would have new members gathering with them to worship.

Jim marveled at the intricate plan God had laid out for them that day. By His hand He had brought them along that little jungle path, leading them to the thatched-roof house church and the surrounding community where they could preach the gospel to the villagers in answer to this one woman's prayers.

A Letter to the Island of Youth

Off the coast of Cuba is a large island called the Island of Youth. There are over 50,000 people there, as well as a handful of churches. Dan and his team, in order to partner with one of these churches in ministry, were planning to fly from Havana, Cuba, out to this island.

But the only airplane flying to the island was a 1939 DC-3—a model that still used twin propellers. It was barely hanging together, and there were no seatbelts inside. The team crowded into the plane, several none-too-happy to be betting their lives on this rickety piece of metal.

Rattling and tilting, the plane lifted off and sped out over the water towards the Island of Youth. The thin metal wings trembled in the air currents and the propellers whirred noisily as the battered old plane dropped and rose and then dropped again, seeming as though every moment it was going to plunge into the waves. By the time the airplane bounced down on the rutted runway, every passenger had said more than a few prayers for survival.

When they had safely disembarked, Dan led the team to the church where they would be working with the local believers. There the Cubans welcomed the North Americans and shared their vision of planting several more churches in the area around them. The e3 team was excited to begin helping the Cuban believers reach their goal.

As was their custom, Dan and his team met up with their interpreters and went out into the streets. They walked from house to house, sharing the gospel and praying for the people who answered the doors.

At one house, Dan knocked on the door and was greeted by a lighter-skinned woman. She looked at Dan and his interpreter and said politely, "Hello. What can I do for you?"

Dan stared at her in surprise. She spoke perfect British English; there would be no need to speak through an interpreter here. They began talking, and the lady introduced herself as Maria Rice. Her 17-year-old daughter, Jacqueline, also spoke English well. Both of them had been taught English by Maria's mother, who was from Great Britain and had lived with them for a time. Maria and her daughter were of mixed race: Cuban and Caucasian. Because of this, they felt like outsiders in their community. They had no relatives in Cuba and few friends. It was very lonely.

Dan shared the gospel with them, and after listening and asking Dan a few questions, both Maria and Jacqueline prayed to receive Christ.

"Is there anything you would like me to pray for you?" Dan asked afterwards.

Maria looked across at her daughter. "Yes, there is," she said. She turned to Dan. "We are very alone here. Since the revolution, we have not seen or heard from any of our family in the United States, Australia, or Great Britain. We would love to at least have some word from them. Could you pray for this?"

"Of course," Dan said, reaching for their hands. They all bowed their heads, and Dan prayed that somehow, God would allow this mother and daughter to receive news from their relatives so far away.

The next day, as Dan was preparing to go out for another day of ministry, one of the Cuban leaders told him, "I'm sorry, but we're one interpreter short today."

"That's alright," Dan said. "Let my interpreter go with one of the other team members."

Then Dan began to pray about what he should do. Without an interpreter, he couldn't share the gospel. "Lord, please lead me," he prayed. "Amen." As he knelt quietly, the Holy Spirit prodded his memory.

"Of course," Dan whispered. "Maria and Jacqueline."

Dan went back to Maria's house, where he asked if she or her daughter would mind interpreting for him that day. Jacqueline was away, but Maria happily agreed to go with him. They went to a nearby town, and as Dan climbed out of the jeep and grabbed his backpack, he remembered: one of the e3 staff back in the USA had given him a couple letters to take to the Island of Youth.

With over 50,000 people on the island, Dan would have no way of knowing to whom to deliver them. But Maria might.

Dan pulled a letter out of his bag. "Would you happen to know who this person is?"

Maria glanced at the envelope, and shook her head. "I'm sorry, but I don't."

Dan dug out the second letter and both of them looked down at the address.

> To: Maria and Jacqueline Rice

There was complete silence. Slowly Maria reached out and took the letter with trembling hands. For a long moment she simply stared at it, reading the names again and again as if she couldn't believe her eyes.

Eventually she turned the envelope over and tore it open. Inside was a carefully folded paper, with a handwritten note. Maria's lips moved in a transfixed whisper as she read the words: "Maria and Jacqueline, I don't even know if you are alive, but if you are, we want you to know—you are loved deeply and missed terribly. We hope we will see you again someday."

She looked up quickly, wiping tears from her eyes. Before she could speak again, she read the words three or four more times. With each moment her smile grew wider, until at last she pressed the letter to her heart and reached for Dan's hand. "Thank you," she said, her voice hushed with awe, "Thank you for praying for us. God has heard."

The letter was from Maria's long lost relatives, who were now living in San Diego, California.

Dan shook Maria's hand warmly, still trying to comprehend the miracle himself. It was statistically impossible for anything like this to happen. Over 50,000 people on this island, and two letters from the United States. Hundreds of houses, and Dan had walked up to Maria's. Many things she and her daughter could have asked for, and they had begged God to let them have word from their relatives.

Even if Dan had known then that he had the letter, he couldn't have known that they would make that prayer request. This one day that Dan hadn't had an interpreter had caused him to return to their home and discover that God had already sent word to the Island of Youth, even before He'd been asked. Dan reveled in the goodness of God. What a joy it was to witness Maria and Jacqueline come to faith in Christ—and then to have them instantly see God answer their prayers.

Five-Minute-Old Believers

It was a year later on the Island of Youth in Cuba. Once again, Dan didn't have an interpreter—and neither Maria nor Jacqueline was free.

"Lord," Dan prayed before he left the house, "Would you show me how to find another interpreter?"

Dan could think of nothing else to do, so he started up the Jeep and drove out of the neighborhood. He prayed again as he drove, "Please Lord, show me an interpreter!"

A few miles later, Dan rolled into an unfamiliar town. He drove slowly down one of the streets, looking around him for anything that would explain why he had been led here. Then he saw a Cuban man walking past on the opposite side of the road.

"Hey!" Dan called out the window. "How are you?"

"Fine! Why?" the man shouted back—in English.

Aha! Dan thought. *An interpreter!*

The man walked over, and Dan explained the situation. Now the man wasn't a Christian, but he did know the Christian pastor in town. So the man, José, climbed into the Jeep and directed Dan down the street to the pastor's house.

Dan met the pastor and instantly struck up a friendship. In a very short time, Dan had formed his own mini-ministry team—himself, the Cuban pastor, and José, who agreed to tag along for the day. They all drove out to the village where Dan and his friends were working.

The reason Dan and the team had come to Cuba was because the church at La Victoria, where the mayor had been saved, now wanted to plant a daughter church in a village 17 kilometers away. Dan and the others were partnering with them to see their vision realized. In this village 17 kilometers away, there was a Christian woman who had to walk that great distance just to come to church. She desperately wanted a church planted where she lived. So both the La Victoria church and the faithful woman were overjoyed to be starting ministry in this village with the help of Dan's team.

Dan and the pastor and the interpreter arrived at the village and began going down the streets sharing the gospel with whomever they met. As they went from house-to-house, they met two teenage sisters who were willing to listen to what Dan had to say. Their names were Dayana and Maricela, 15 and 19 years old, respectively. Dan opened his EvangeCube, and he and the interpreter shared the entire gospel story, finishing with how the girls could be saved by Jesus.

When he had closed the cube, Maricela said softly, "I want to pray to Him."

Her sister, Dayana, wasn't ready to trust Christ yet.

Dan and the pastor bowed their heads with Maricela, and she asked Jesus to take away her sins and be her Lord and Savior. The smile on Maricela's face as she raised her eyes was dazzling.

A few minutes later, Dayana and Maricela's 17-year-old sister, Veronica, walked into the room. She sat down quietly as Dan talked with Maricela about the next steps in her life with Christ.

"After we're saved, one of the most important things we are to do is to share our faith with others," Dan said. He showed Maricela the back of the EvangeCube, which tells new Christians how to grow in their relationship with Christ—by praying, studying God's word, fellowshipping with other believers, and sharing the gospel.

Dan gently handed Maricela the EvangeCube. "Why don't you share the gospel with your sister?" he suggested, motioning to Veronica.

Maricela looked up at Dan, her eyes wide. Dan nodded encouragingly.

Taking a shaky breath, Maricela turned to Veronica and began telling her about Jesus, using the EvangeCube. She carefully went through each panel, fumbling a bit when she rearranged the cube. As the pastor gently helped her along, she became more comfortable, and when she reached the end of the presentation she was beaming.

Veronica listened, captivated by the story of God's love. "I want Jesus to save me," she said earnestly.

"So do I," Dayana said suddenly. She had been listening silently as the gospel was shared again, and now she wiped tears from her eyes and smiled at her older sisters. The look of joy and relief that filled Maricela's face was precious. She ran to her sisters and hugged them both tightly. Then the three sisters knelt together as Veronica and Dayana asked Jesus to be their Savior.

As soon as the girls had said, "Amen," their 13-year-old brother, Rafael, came home. He smiled shyly at the visitors and sat down next to Veronica.

Just as he had with Maricela, Dan handed the EvangeCube to Veronica. "Your brother also needs to hear," he said quietly.

With the pastor's help, Veronica shared the gospel with Rafael. He listened with a hungry look on his face, and when she had finished, he too asked Jesus to save him.

The four siblings were still laughing and crying together when their mother came into the room. Dan passed the EvangeCube to Rafael, the newest believer. Like his sisters, he took the cube nervously, but when he started to share the gospel he spoke boldly and with confidence. His mother slowly dropped down into a chair, listening in wonder to the message of hope her son was giving. Rafael asked if she wanted to pray to Jesus. Choking back a sob, his mother nodded silently. Together, the children knelt with her and she received Jesus as her Savior.

Within minutes of accepting the gift of salvation, the new believers had already shared the Good News. The very next day, when the father came home, the sisters, brother, and their mother all shared the gospel with him—and he also accepted Christ.

This family of young believers started a house church in their home with others who had been saved, and thus a new church was planted in the village 17 kilometers from La Victoria. The woman who had walked so far to attend church now lived three doors down from the nearest congregation!

A Symbol of Salvation

It was Dan and the team's last night in Cuba at the end of an amazing time of outreach and growth. Two hundred seventy-six people had come to Christ and seven churches had been planted. That evening there was a celebration service at the Cuban church, where the local Christians could come together to be encouraged and to praise the Lord for all He had done. The pastor asked Dan to give the final message. Of course Dan was happy to do so.

When evening came, the church was packed with over 700 people. Outside were another several hundred, unable to squeeze through the doors but pressing close to the walls. They peered through the windows or listened at the crack in the door, trying to catch the message.

In front of this huge, eager crowd, Dan was preparing to stand up to speak. But as Dan rose from his chair, the Cuban pastor grabbed his arm.

"There are several Cuban officials here in the audience," the pastor whispered in Dan's ear. "Be careful what you say. Since you're supposed to be tourists, not evangelists."

Dan had had a message in mind—but in light of this new information, that message wouldn't work at all. Slowly, he stood up in front of the crowd, scanning the room. He wondered which faces belonged to the Cuban officials who would be listening.

Tourist, not evangelist, Dan reminded himself. He took a deep breath. This task seemed im-

171

possible. How could he give a message to the Christians, speaking about the great mission work they had seen, without revealing that the team had been evangelizing?

Then the Holy Spirit brought a passage of Scripture into Dan's mind: "And you will even be brought before governors and kings for My sake, as a testimony to them and to the Gentiles. But when they hand you over, do not worry about how or what you are to say, for it will be given to you in that hour what you are to say. For it is not you who speak, but it is the Spirit of your Father who speaks in you" (Matthew 10:18-20).

Alright, Lord, Dan prayed. *You speak through me!*

Earlier that week the team had taken a day off from ministry to go play on the beach, in order to keep up the appearance of being tourists. As Dan stood wondering what he would preach on for this service, he remembered the beach trip—and the Holy Spirit gave him a new message.

"It has been a great week," Dan began cheerily. "We got to go scuba diving recently, and the underwater world truly is beautiful. It was so different from being on the shore. And it reminded me that as Christians, we are to be different from the regular world. We are to be ambassadors for the King." The people nodded, listening thoughtfully.

Now Dan was going to move to outreach. *Please let them understand*, he prayed.

"The fishing on this island is great!" Dan exclaimed. "We saw *seven* fishing boats go out onto the water this week. And the Cubans we saw fishing caught *two hundred and seventy-six* fish! That's a lot."

The Christians suddenly burst into applause, cheering and shouting. Dan grinned. They had gotten it. Of course, the Cubans which Dan had seen "fishing" were catching people, not fish. And those seven fishing boats were the seven churches which had been started.

Dan spoke a little more about fish, and swimming, and other tourist activities, just to be safe. Then, somewhere in the assembly, a little child cried.

Dan looked out over the crowd. "Could you hold your child up, please?" he asked the mother.

The mother raised her tiny child in her arms. Dan gestured to the infant. "What would happen to this little baby if he had no one to take care of him?" Dan asked the people.

A faint murmur stirred the room, and then someone called, "He would die."

Dan nodded. "Yes. But he has his mother to nurture him, raise him, and instruct him. So he will continue to grow." Dan smiled at the mother, and she gently lowered the child back into her protective embrace.

"In the same way, if a believer is not trained, guided and encouraged, he will not grow." Dan addressed the Cuban Christians who had been working with the team that week. "You have a responsibility to disciple the young Christians who do not know as much as you do, and to continue to lead them in worship and prayer and studies of God's Word."

The Cubans called out their assent and promised not to abandon the new believers, but to fulfill their duty to mentor and lead them.

Dan finished his message with a prayer, and then sat back down. He was sweating slightly. The whole time, in the back of his mind, he had been thinking about speaking carefully so as to avoid causing any trouble. However, he thought the talk had gone well. There were no unhappy faces in the room.

Two of his team members spoke next, sharing their personal testimonies. Afterwards the

Cuban pastor stood up. As a national, it was politically allowable for him to extend an invitation for salvation, while Dan could not. The pastor shared the gospel, explaining how anyone could have a personal relationship with God through Jesus Christ. He asked those who had not yet believed, but who wanted that relationship, to follow him in a simple prayer of salvation. When he said "Amen," he asked if anyone had accepted Christ that night.

Many of the people at the service were already Christians. But several others around the room raised their hands, proclaiming that they had asked Jesus to forgive their sins and that He was now their Lord and Savior.

Then from outside in the night, a hand appeared. It pushed through the window, the fingers stretched full out, reaching into the warmth and light of the building. Another soul, listening from the other side of the wall, had accepted Christ into his life that night—and he wanted everyone to know.

Have you read the original
I Heard Good News Today?
It contains 93 short, true stories kids love depicting
the chronological and geographical spread of the gospel.

www.UnveilinGLORY.com/Bookstore

Make sure you read
I Heard Good News Today 2: Big Life.
These true 21st Century stories will amaze you
with what God is doing globally!

www.UnveilinGLORY.com/Bookstore

For Children in
Kindergarten through 2nd Grade:
Adventures In Obedience

For Children in Grades 2 - 5:

Cat and Dog Attitudes

The Children's Workbook

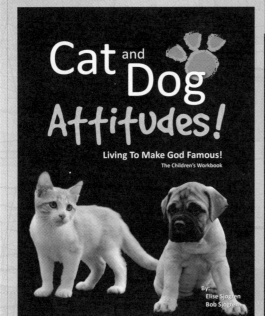

The Parent's Guidebook

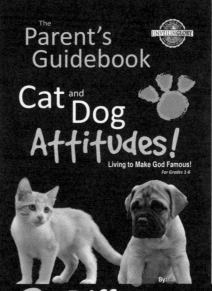

A Full Color Cartoon Book for Kids

I Heard Good News Today 2: Big Life

Cartoons on God's Glory

Elise's Teaching On the Glory of God In Nature!

For Children in Grades 3-5:
Kids and The Kingdom!